EMII SELECTED POEMS

NOTES

including
- *Life and Background*
- *Introduction*
- *The Texts of Dickinson's Poems and Letters*
- *Dickinson's Poetic Methods*
- *The Poems*
    Nature: Scene and Meaning
    Poetry, Art, and Imagination
    Friendship, Love, and Society
    Death, Immortality, and Religion
- *Brief Comments on Forty Additional Poems*
- *Questions for Review and Writing*
- *Selected Bibliography*
- *Index of First Lines*

by
Mordecai Marcus, Ph.D.
Department of English
University of Nebraska

INCORPORATED

LINCOLN, NEBRASKA   68501

Editor

Gary Carey, M.A.
University of Colorado

Consulting Editor

James L. Roberts, Ph.D.
Department of English
University of Nebraska

Cliffs Notes, Inc.   Lincoln, Nebraska

CONTENTS

EMILY DICKINSON NOTES

LIFE OF THE AUTHOR

Emily Dickinson was born in Amherst, Massachusetts, on December 10, 1830, and died there some fifty-five years later on May 15, 1886. With the exception of a few visits to Boston, Philadelphia, and Washington, D.C., and some nine months at school at South Hadley, Massachusetts, she spent her whole life in Amherst, most of it in the large meadow-surrounded house called the Dickinson Homestead, across the street from a cemetery. From 1840 to 1855, she lived with her family in a house on North Pleasant Street, after which they returned to the Homestead. She never married, and she lived in comfortable dependence on her well-to-do father and his estate, though she did more than her share of household chores while creating a large body of poems and letters.

Amherst, a farm-based community, grew in her lifetime from about 2,700 to about 4,200 inhabitants. It was the seat of Amherst College, a citadel of Protestant orthodoxy, and later of Massachusetts Agricultural and Mechanical College (now University of Massachusetts). Though somewhat isolated, Amherst had a good private academy, a rich but mixed cultural tradition of reading the Bible, Shakespeare, and the classics; and, as the nineteenth century progressed, contemporary American authors and a large amount of popular and sentimental literature became current there. Social life was confined largely to church affairs, college receptions, agricultural shows, and such private socializing as walking, carriage riding, and discussing books. Newspapers and magazines from Springfield and Boston brought current literature and opinion, serious and ephemeral, to the more literate. The Dickinson clan were old Yankee stock, tolerant of such religious dissidence as Unitarianism and Roman Catholicism, but deeply rooted in the orthodox Protestant tradition as it lived on in their own Congregational church (and the Presbyterian church), still actively Calvinistic and requiring public profession of faith for membership. Waves of religious enthusiasm and conversion swept through Amherst, especially during Emily Dickinson's early years, and gathered up her friends and members of her family, but never her.

Little is known of Emily Dickinson's earliest years. She spent four years at a primary school and then attended Amherst Academy from 1840 to 1847, somewhat irregularly because of poor health. She wrote imaginatively for school publications but none of these writings survive. Her intense letters to friends and classmates show a variety of tones, especially in her reluctance to embrace Christ and join the church and in her anticipations and fears about the prospect of a married life. The world, as she understood the idea, was more dear to her than the renunciations which conversion seemed to require, and quite possibly she sensed something false or soft-minded in the professions of others. In a period of rigorous living conditions, without the benefits of modern medicine, life spans were shorter than ours, and Dickinson suffered the early deaths of many acquaintances and dear friends. She witnessed several deaths, doubtlessly impressed and shocked by the Puritan doctrine that looked for signs of election and salvation in the demeanor of the dying and especially in their willingness to die.

During this period, she was fond of, or attached to, two older men, Leonard Humphrey (1824-50), the young principal of Amherst Academy, and Benjamin Franklin Newton (1821-53), a law student in her father's office. Newton, a Unitarian and something of an Emersonian, discussed literature, ideas, and religion with her, and praised her early poetic efforts. After he left her father's office and moved to Worcester, he married and soon died of tuberculosis. Dickinson evidently felt a warm, sisterly affection for him, and on learning of his death, she worried about the state and future of his soul. It was a kind of worry which she would continue to experience throughout the rest of her life about the many people whom she cared for. Romantic inclinations towards Humphrey and Newton seem extremely unlikely for Dickinson, but these men are probably related to the descriptions of several losses in her early poems. In the fall of 1847, Dickinson began the first of a two-year program at Mount Holyoke Female Seminary in South Hadley, where she did not yield to continued pressures to give up the secular world for Christ and join the church. A good student and fond of her classmates and teachers, she suffered homesickness and poor health, and she did not return for the second year.

Her immediate family were probably the most important people in Dickinson's life. Her father, Edward Dickinson (1803-74), a graduate of Yale law college, was a successful lawyer and Amherst's chief citizen by virtue of his imposing personality, his connection with Amherst College (its treasurer), his two terms in the state legislature, his one term in the United States Congress, and his leadership in civic endeavors. A man of unbending demeanor and rectitude, he appears to have had a softer side that he struggled to conceal. It came out in incidents of pleasure in nature, kindliness to people, and the embarrassed desire for more intimacy with his children than he ever allowed himself. He joined the church at the age of fifty. Dickinson expressed her distress over his death in many poems and letters. In some sense, she may have lived in his shadow, but she went her own way and saw him with a critical as well as with a tender eye. He probably appears in some of her poems about deprivation and about explosive behavior. It is unlikely that he made any explicit attempts to keep either of his daughters from marrying, although he probably did communicate a sense of his need for their presence and support.

A clear picture of Dickinson's mother, Emily Norcross Dickinson (1804-82), is difficult to formulate. She seems to have been dignified, conventional, reasonably intelligent, and probably subservient to her husband. She suffered periods of poor health, probably of emotional origin, and her health was shattered by her husband's death. Dickinson and her sister, Lavinia, cared for her as an invalid for the last four years of her life, during which Dickinson's affection for her greatly increased. Dickinson's declaration to T. W. Higginson, her chief literary correspondent, that she "never had a mother" is poetically exaggerated.

Dickinson's sister and brother, Lavinia (1833-99) and William Austin, known always as Austin, (1829-95), were close to her all her life. Lavinia was a vivacious, pretty, and clever girl, but not particularly intellectual, although she had a reputation for having a sharp tongue. She seems to have rejected several offers of marriage, possibly in order to remain Dickinson's lifelong companion. Fiercely protective of her elder sister, she probably tried to shield the ever more reclusive Dickinson, and she may have understood Dickinson's need to have time and privacy for her poems. More imaginative and intellectual than his father, Austin had an artistic side and was interested in new ideas. After finishing law school and marrying, he succumbed to his father's pressures for him not to leave Amherst for

Chicago, became his father's law partner, and settled for life in a house across the street from the Dickinson home. Partly because of Dickinson's influence, he married Susan Gilbert, who had long been a close friend of Dickinson's. The marriage was unhappy, and its increasing tensions were probably visible to those in the house across the street.

Dickinson's relationship with her sister-in-law is very revealing and is relevant to these Notes. It was in the early 1850s that Susan Gilbert, (later Dickinson) (1830-1913), an orphan, came to live with relatives in Amherst and became Dickinson's dearest friend. They shared books, ideas, and friends. After a stormy courtship, Susan married Austin in 1856. A woman of attractiveness, intelligence, powerful social demeanor, and a stinging tongue, Susan became the social leader of Amherst. Her relationship with Dickinson remained highly ambivalent, Dickinson suffering from Susan's sarcasm mixed with her tenderness and also from Susan's pressures to make her submit to conventional religion. Dickinson wrote warm and revealing letters and poems to Susan but seems to have become quite disillusioned with her, though her fondness for Austin and Susan's three children and her sympathy for her brother kept her bonds with Susan partly whole. The death of Gilbert Dickinson (1875-83), Austin and Susan's youngest child, was a terrible blow to Dickinson.

During the 1850s, Dickinson made the most of her few travels outside Amherst, visiting Boston, Washington, and Philadelphia, but she was becoming more reclusive; she stopped attending church services (she had been a keen observer and often sarcastic commentator on sermons), and she spent much of her time writing poems. Towards the end of the decade, Dickinson seemed to be approaching several emotional crises. In her early twenties, she had experienced some normal social attentions from young men, but probably none of them constituted what one could call courtship. In 1858, 1861, and 1862 (these dates are approximate), she wrote draft copies of three fervent letters to someone whom she addressed as "Master," while calling herself "Daisy." The letters are anguished descriptions of a guilty, rejected, and subservient love. Quite possibly, these letters were never sent. They are the strongest available evidence that a desperate and impossible love was the chief source of her crises, although there is no proof of it.

Among the many candidates advanced as Dickinson's secret love, two men have been singled out as being most likely: the

Reverend Charles Wadsworth (1814-82) of Philadelphia and San Francisco, and Samuel Bowles (1826-78), editor of the Springfield *Republican* and a lifelong friend of the Edward and Austin Dickinson families. Charles Wadsworth was a successful orthodox preacher — sober but imaginative, rigorous yet tender. Dickinson probably heard him preach in Philadelphia in 1855. He visited her in Amherst and of his correspondence with Dickinson, only a short letter from him to her survives, revealing a pastoral concern for an unspecified distress. After his death, Dickinson wrote of him in various endearing terms, calling him her "dearest earthly friend." Happily married and the father of several children, Wadsworth must have been completely unaware of any romantic attachment which Dickinson may have felt for him. The fact that Wadsworth's San Francisco church was called Calvary and that many of Dickinson's love poems employ religious allusions have suggested but do not prove that she was romantically infatuated with Wadsworth.

Samuel Bowles is a more likely candidate for the person addressed in Dickinson's so-called Master letters. An extremely handsome and worldly man, Bowles numbered many women among his friends, much to his wife's pain. A frequent visitor at the Dickinsons, he may have tempted Emily to plead with him for recognition of her poetic ability, a recognition which he was quite unable to give. Emily Dickinson's letters to him bear significant similarities to the Master letters, and she sent him many poems, including "Title divine — is mine!" (1072); this one was accompanied with a note, which may imply that in her imagination he was her husband. Various details of the lives and travels of both Wadsworth and Bowles fit selectively into Dickinson's comments on separations and losses which she suffered, but others do not. Possibly Dickinson worshipped in her imagination a composite of these two men or a version of someone else who cannot be identified. Her emotional crises of the early 1860s may also stem from her fear about the condition of her eyes (which, in turn, may have been of emotional origin), fears for her sanity in connection with these difficulties and with family instabilities, or a combination of love-desperation with all of these frustrations. She may also have been desperate because no one could recognize her poetic gifts. Her increasing reclusiveness and her continually wearing white dresses may be chiefly related to the idea that in spirit she was married to someone; this may suggest that in addition to all these conflicts, there was a need for time and privacy for her writing and an increasing conviction that she derived more satisfaction from living in the world of her poems than in ordinary society. In any case, her poetic productivity from 1861 to about 1866 continued at an astonishing rate. The figure of an unattainable lover looms large in her poems, but it is probably a mistake to think that a frustrated love was the chief cause of her becoming a poet. Nevertheless, one must grant that her writing served as an emotional catharsis and as a healing therapy for her, which contributes to its appeal.

Emily Dickinson's chief attempt to establish contact with the literary world and gain recognition for her poems began in 1862 when she wrote a letter to Thomas Wentworth Higginson (1823-1911) and sent him the first of many packets of poems. Dickinson was responding to advice that Higginson had offered to young writers in the *Atlantic Monthly*. Higginson was a minister, editor, writer, soldier, and a champion of liberal causes. Emily Dickinson's correspondence with him, which continued almost until her death, is the most important part of her correspondence, and Higginson, who visited her in 1870 and 1873, has left the most detailed reports on her conversation that we have. Higginson recognized in Dickinson a sensitive, gifted, and imaginative person, but he could not see her work as poetry; he described it as beautiful thoughts and words, and he cautioned her against early publication, trying to steer her towards conventional form and expression, and trying to draw her into society. She pretended to accept all his criticism and to plead for a continued tutor-mentor relationship, but she seems to have recognized all his limitations and to have drawn sustenance from his personal, rather than from his literary support. Higginson probably appears in a number of Dickinson's poems about the relationship of artist and audience. After Dickinson's death, Higginson helped edit her poems, and their popular success greatly advanced his opinion of them.

During Emily Dickinson's lifetime, only seven of her poems appeared in print – all unsigned and all altered and damaged by editors. She had probably agreed to only a few of these publications. Five of these poems appeared in Bowles's *Springfield Republican*. One appeared in 1878 in the anonymous anthology *A Masque of Poets*, surely as a result of the persuasion of Dickinson's only other important literary friend, Helen Hunt Jackson (1830-85), who, as Helen Fiske, had been among Dickinson's childhood friends in Amherst. After the death of her first husband, Helen Hunt, later Jackson, became a successful poet and novelist (famous for *Ramona*, 1884). In the 1870s, she wrote to and visited Dickinson, became convinced of her greatness as a poet, and tried to persuade her to publish. Her only success, however, was to persuade Dickinson to contribute "Success is counted sweetest" (67) to *A Masque of Poets*, but she told Dickinson that she was a great poet, and Dickinson's correspondence shows a warm affection for her.

The other important relationship of Emily Dickinson's later years was her reciprocated love for Judge Otis P. Lord (1812-84), a friend of her father's, who became Dickinson's close friend after he was widowed in 1877. Dickinson's letters to him are fervent with bashful love. He seems to have proposed, and she seems to have refused in the name of her persisting sense that fulfillment would have overwhelmed her. Lord's death in 1884 seems to have shocked Dickinson into a rapid physical decline. According to some writers, he appears in a few of her late poems.

After her withdrawal from the world in the early 1860s, Dickinson's life revolved around her correspondence, her poetry, and her household duties. She remained a faithful daughter and sister, and in her own terms, she was a faithful friend to many to whom she related chiefly through letters. Her later reclusiveness may have approached a certain pathological state, as evidenced by her turning friends away and sometimes conversing and listening to music through only slightly opened doors. But Dickinson constantly insisted that she did not suffer from her isolation and that she felt deeply fulfilled and in intimate contact with the world. Her correspondence with Higginson probably convinced her that her poems would find no significant or sympathetic audience during her lifetime, for though she protested to Higginson that she did not want publication, it is evident that she wanted to make her relatives proud of her work after she died, and her combination of pride and resignation probably stemmed from her awareness of her great gift and her frustration that so many people were as mystified by her poems as by her talk. Many of the poems give eloquent testimony that she longed for an audience. As luck would have it, her poems survived. But their struggle for adequate publication, understanding, and recognition almost parallels her inner life in its complexity.

INTRODUCTION

Enormously popular since the early piecemeal publication of her poems, Emily Dickinson has enjoyed an ever-increasing critical reputation, and she is now widely regarded as one of America's best poets. These Notes focus on clarification of some eighty-five of her poems, chosen and emphasized largely according to the frequency of their appearance in eight standard anthologies, where the average number of her poems is fifty. These poems also seem to offer an excellent representation of her themes and power. In a final section to these Notes, additional poems are commented on briefly.

In face of the difficulty of many of her poems and the bafflingly diffuse and contradictory general impression made by her work and personality, Dickinson's popularity is a great tribute to her genius. Her poems are often difficult because of their unusual compression, unconventional grammar, their strange diction and strained figures of speech, and their often generalized symbolism and allegory. She took up baffling and varied attitudes towards a great many questions about life and death, and she expressed these in a great variety of tones. The speaker in these individual poems is often hard to identify. In many poems, she preferred to conceal the specific causes and nature of her deepest feelings, especially experiences of suffering, and her subjects flow so much into one another in language and conception that often it is difficult to tell if she is writing about people or God, nature or society, spirit or art. One often suspects that many such subjects are being treated simultaneously. Furthermore, her condensed style and monotonous rhythms make sustained reading of her work difficult. The flagging attention that results can contribute to misperception and hasty judgment. Nevertheless, since her poems are mutually illuminating, the reader may face the choice of trying to learn much from a generous selection or trying to concentrate on the essentials of a smaller number.

Fortunately, common sense and expert guidance can offer new insights into this maze. Usually, biographical information is useful in interpreting a poet according to the degree of strangeness in the situations and states of mind which the poet portrays. It is true that Emily Dickinson's themes are universal, but her particular vantage points tend to be very personal; she rebuilt her world *inside* the products of her poetic imagination. This is why some knowledge of her life and her cast of mind is essential for illuminating much of her work. Such knowledge, however, must always be used with caution and tact, for otherwise it can lead to quick judgments, simplifications, and distortions. Understanding of her work is helped even more by recognizing some of her fundamental *patterns* of subject matter and treatment, particularly her contrasting attitudes and the ways in which her subjects blend into one another. Such patterns may – and for the Dickinson expert must – include material from her life and letters, but this approach requires a continual awareness that, like her poems, her letters were written for specific effects *on* their readers (they were often drafted), and they are often even more vague than her poems on parallel subjects. The Dickinson devotee will eventually emerge with a multi-faceted and large-scale conception of her poetic personality. Fortunately, a smaller-scale and yet rich conception is possible for readers who immerse themselves in only fifty or a hundred of her poems. One of the joys of such reading, very particular to Emily Dickinson, is that the effort to keep such a conception flexible will bring added pleasure with fresh visits to her work.

Nothing, however, will help quite as much as careful reading of her own words, sentences, stanzas, and whole poems. Particular attention should be given to grasping the sense of her whole sentences, filling in missing elements, straightening out inverted word order, and expanding the sense of telescoped phrases and metaphors. Perhaps most important for understanding Emily Dickinson is the testing of one's conceptions of the tone or tones of individual poems and relating them to other poems and to one's own emotional ideas and feelings.

Scholarly aids are generously available but not equally reliable. Outdated and wrong-headed materials are sometimes recommended, but the wise beginning student should disregard these resources until he or she has a firmer foundation to build on. For a full understanding of Emily Dickinson, a reading of her complete poems and letters is essential. For a more than generous sample of her best poetry, *Final Harvest* is outstanding. The early biographies by Bianchi, Pollitt, and Taggard should be avoided. The biographies by Whicher, Chase, and particularly the biography by Johnson give accounts reliable up to a point. The biography of Sewall outdates all of these in its thoroughness and use of new materials, but it is

14

cumbersome in its bulk and organization. Excellent critical books and articles abound but are frequently one-sided. Often after one has immersed himself or herself in Emily Dickinson thoroughly, one's own intellectual and emotional responses and implications are as genuine and accurate as the scholars' evaluations.

THE TEXTS OF DICKINSON'S POEMS AND LETTERS

After Emily Dickinson died, she left behind several drawersful of poems in various states of completion: fair copies, semi-final drafts, and rough drafts, all strangely punctuated and capitalized. Her handwriting is difficult, and many manuscripts list alternate choices for words, lines, and stanzas. In the 1890s, T. W. Higginson and Mabel Loomis Todd began publishing some of her poems in *First Series* (1890), *Second Series* (1891), and, by Mrs. Todd alone, *Third Series* (1896); these volumes included 449 poems. In order to create popular public acceptance, they often corrected grammar, conventionalized punctuation, improved rhymes, omitted stanzas, and supplied titles. In succeeding decades, Martha Dickinson Bianchi and A. L. Hampson edited several more small volumes and then collected many of the remaining poems into *The Poems of Emily Dickinson*, 1937. They took fewer liberties with the texts, but they misread many words in the manuscripts. In 1945, Millicent Todd Bingham issued her completion of her mother, M. L. Todd's, editing of another 668 poems, under the title *Bolts of Melody*, a carefully edited but also repunctuated text. (To repunctuate Dickinson is often to re-interpret her poems.) In 1955, Thomas H. Johnson edited from all known manuscripts *The Poems of Emily Dickinson, Including Variant Readings*. This edition, known as the Johnson text, attempted to report the manuscripts with complete accuracy and arranged the poems according to their dates of composition, as estimated by Emily Dickinson's changing handwriting, which helped establish Dickinson's yearly rates of composition. This volume also supplied poem numbers which are now almost universally used with first lines to identify each poem. This edition contains 1775 poems and fragments. When faced with textual variants, Johnson chose words and lines listed first, but he reported all the others in footnotes. In 1960, Johnson simplified the variorum edition into a single volume, reader's edition, *The Complete Poems of Emily Dickinson*, recently reissued in a reduced-type paperback edition. The single volume edition occasionally departs from the textual choices of the variorum. In 1961, Johnson issued *Final Harvest*, a selection of 575 poems. Early printings of the one-volume edition and of *Final Harvest* contain a number of misprints. As for Dickinson's letters, a body of work which many critics believe to be as valuable as her poetry because of its imagery and ideas, two editions of selections from Emily Dickinson's letters appeared under M. L. Todd's editorship in 1894 and 1931. In 1958, T. H. Johnson gathered all known letters into the three-volume *The Letters of Emily Dickinson*. A number of the best known early critical essays on Emily Dickinson, including those by Conrad Aiken, Allen Tate, and Yvor Winters, quote from the sometimes mangled pre-Johnson texts. Most contemporary anthologies employ the Johnson texts, but the earlier editions still reside on library shelves and two selections of Emily Dickinson's poems that remain in print, edited respectively by R. N. Linscott and J. M. Brinnin, use pre-Johnson texts either wholly or substantially, sometimes misleadingly for the reader.

DICKINSON'S IDEAS

Emily Dickinson's major ideas are readily available to us in her poems and letters, but on first reading, they form complicated and often contradictory patterns. This is not surprising; her world was insular and small, and she was highly introspective. In addition, her work has its roots in the culture and society of her times, but though these can be explored extensively and many parallels can be established between her statements and various literary and religious documents, the poems create more mutual illumination than does Emily Dickinson's background itself. Orthodox Protestantism in its Calvinistic guise was the major underpinning of nineteenth-century Amherst society, though it was undergoing shocks and assaults. This New England faith, often called Puritanism, was based on the idea of man as being sinful and unregenerate and completely at the mercy of a loving but arbitrary God. Salvation was by predestined election (it lay entirely in the will of God), but acceptance of God's will, and renunciation of the world for Christ, were paramount for proof of piety and peace of soul. Worldly success and religious faith were taken as signs of salvation but not as its causes. In Dickinson's time, this faith was wearing thin, and material success had long replaced deep piety as the real standard for recognizing the elect. This thinning out of faith helped create the ideas of New England Unitarianism and Transcendentalism. Unitarianism having watered down the emotional components of religion, the transcendentalism of Ralph Waldo Emerson and others elevated man's spirituality, self-development, and union with the stream of nature to the level of the divine, without ever quite denying the Godhead. The Puritans had seen God's will everywhere in the signs of nature. In Emerson's footsteps, Whitman, Thoreau, and certainly Emily Dickinson tended to see man's spirit manifested or symbolized in nature, though Dickinson often saw only the human mind reading its feelings into nature. Dickinson was aware of and troubled by the admitted and surreptitious breakdown of faith in her time, and she was dubious of all measures to shore it up. She drew sustenance from new ideas, but sometimes found them shallow. She rejected old ideas, but found in them much emotional correspondence to her own set of mind.

For Dickinson, the crucial religious question was the survival of the soul after death. She rejected absolutely the idea of man's innate depravity; she favored the Emersonian partial reversal of Puritanism that conceived greatness of soul as the source of immortality. The God of the Bible was alternately real, mythical, and unlikely to her. She could neither accept nor reject His assurance of a life beyond death, and her doubts pushed her faintly in the direction of transcendental naturalism or towards mere terror of dissolution. She declares, alternately, faith and doubt with equal vehemence, surely as much because of her own struggles with the idea of and need for fulfillment as because of any intellectual battlement. Her sarcastic comments on the God of the Bible are not necessarily jocular. She was independent minded, but she did not shift her stance in her letters to suit her recipients, nor in her poems presumably, to suit her moods; she was interested primarily in her poetic momentum.

In some sense, Dickinson is almost always a religious poet – if her concerns with human perception, suffering, growth, and fulfillment as directed towards something permanent can be called religious concerns. These concerns are as important for her as are death and immortality, and though they have doctrinal and literary sources, they come chiefly from her observations and reflections on life.

Dickinson's reading was comparatively wide, and she knew both the essays and poems of Emerson, as well as Shakespeare, the Bible, the works of George Eliot, Hawthorne, the Brownings, and other earlier and contemporary classics. She alludes often to the Bible, and her combination of dense metaphors with everyday reality sometimes resembles Shakespeare's. However, both the Emersonian cast of her mind, which we will note in several poems, and her darker Puritan strain, were as much a part of the general atmosphere of her culture as of its specific beliefs and its reading matter. Dickinson's literary culture overlaps her religious culture, but the parallels they provide to her work are usually more incidental than revealing.

Although she prided herself on her indifference to broader social concerns, Dickinson does comment occasionally on the social landscape, particularly as it catches her satirical eye. Nature appears widely in her work – as a scene of great liveliness and beauty, as the embodiment of the processes of the universe which may resemble the actions of God and the shape of the human mind, and as an endless source of metaphors and symbols for all of her subjects. Nature, for her, is usually bright and dark mystery, only occasionally illuminated by flashes of pantheism and sometimes darkened by hopeless fatality. Her treatment of nature blends into all of her subjects.

The tradition of classifying Dickinson's poems into thematic groupings for analysis and comparison has been unjustly criticized. As we have remarked, it can contribute to simplification and distortion, but it is more illuminating than approaching the poems by categories of technique or periods in her life, and the danger of simplification can be easily met by a persistent testing of her poems against categories; that is, one can always consider the possibility that they have been misplaced or need to be viewed as part of several categories. For these Notes, we have grouped her poems under five major headings, aware that a few major poems may escape such a classification: (1) Nature: Scene and Meaning; (2) Poetry, Art, and Imagination; (3) Friendship, Love, and Society; (4) Suffering and Growth; and (5) Death, Immortality, and Religion.

DICKINSON'S POETIC METHODS

A glance through Dickinson's poems reveals their characteristic external forms as easily as a quick look through Whitman's poems shows us his strikingly different forms. Most of Emily Dickinson's poems are written in short stanzas, mostly quatrains, with short lines, usually rhyming only on the second and fourth lines. Other stanzas employ triplets or pairs of couplets, and a few poems employ longer, looser, and more complicated stanzas. Iambic rhythms dominate, but they are varied and loosened, speeded and slowed, in many ways. A large number of Dickinson's rhymes are what we call partial, slant, or off-rhymes, some of these so faint as to be barely recognizable. She was obviously aware that she was violating convention here, but she stubbornly stuck to her ways. These stanza forms and, to a lesser extent, her poetic rhymes took their chief source from the standard Protestant hymns of her day, largely from those of Isaac Watts.

Dickinson evidently found a convenient mold for her thoughts in these forms, and her use of partial rhyme may have helped her to compose swiftly and to focus on selection of words and metaphors. It is possible that her slant rhymes reflect her emotional tensions (fracture would be a stronger word for it), but most critical attempts to establish clear-cut correlations between types of rhyme and particular moods in her poems are relatively unsuccessful. Nevertheless, these slant rhymes seem consistent with the improvisatory and brooding quality of her mind.

The relative simplicity and monotony of her verse forms contribute to the difficulty of reading Dickinson in large quantities at single sittings, but one never fails to sense and remember her unique poetic genius. Her stanza forms and rhythmical nuances continuously contribute brilliantly to her effects. For example, Dickinson's poems often burst with images and metaphors drawn from many diverse sources. Nature is paramount. Other sources include domestic activities, industry and warfare, and law and economy. Her images sometimes create natural or social scenes but are more likely to create psychological landscapes, generalized scenes, or allegorical scenes. She is like a deep, mysterious mine where one can find many examples of how she blends symbolism and allegory. (Symbolism is the use of real scenes and actions to suggest universal ideas and emotions in addition to the scenes. Allegory is the use of scenes and actions whose structuring is so artificial and unreal that the reader comes to see that they stand for people, scenes, and ideas recognizably different from the representation itself.) This blending of symbolism and allegory in Dickinson's poems is another reason for some readers' difficulty when they encounter her many poems for the first time; yet, Emily Dickinson's evocative powers are paramount: she is always a challenge to the reader.

Besides the great conciseness of language we have already stressed, the most striking signature of Dickinson's style is her blending of the homely and exalted, the trivial and the precious, in her images, metaphors, and scenes. The chief effect that she achieves here is to increase our scrutiny of small-scale things and focus on the texture and significance of large ones. It also serves to permeate her physical world with questions of value. Dickinson's sense of humor and her skepticism help communicate the urgencies of her doubts and need to find faith. Her metaphors are also sometimes telescoped; that is, they incorporate elements so condensed or disparate that they must be elongated, drawn out like a telescope, to reveal the full structure of a picture or an idea.

Dickinson herself told Higginson that the speaker in her poems is *not* herself but a supposed person, thereby anticipating the perhaps too popular modern idea that poems are always spoken by a fictitious person. This provides a very healthy caution for interpreting Dickinson, but this idea should not keep us from using our knowledge of her life and thought to interpret her poems. Of equal importance is the variety of tones throughout her poems, a variety related to the problem of identifying her speakers. The chief tonal problem is distinguishing between ironic and non-ironic voices. Her ironies can be very obvious or very subtle. Clues to irony are often found in the structure of a poem's statements where doubts and reversals reveal earlier ironies. The likelihood that Dickinson was deliberately posing in many of her poems complicates the problem of tone – but her poses are not necessarily sentimental. Awareness of her shifting of masks can help us resist our doubts that she is serious when she adopts a view we dislike. We also need to recognize her possibly fierce ironies when she is denouncing beliefs which we hold precious or when she is reacting in ways we disapprove of. Again, the poems sometimes seem puzzling, yet after a rereading, they are often suddenly illuminating. To paraphrase Dickinson, scrutiny of this problem keeps the mind nimble. Probably she wanted to keep her own and her readers' minds as nimble as possible.

THE POEMS

Nature: Scene and Meaning

Since Emily Dickinson was a child of rural nineteenth-century New England, it is not surprising that the natural scenes and figurative language drawn from it loom very large throughout her work. She had read in the poetry of Wordsworth, Bryant, and Emerson — all products of a Romantic movement that looked for meaning, imagery, and spiritual refreshment in nature. Her roots in a Puritanism that saw God manifested everywhere in nature contributed to her pursuit of personal significance in nature. The New England countryside of her time was still largely untrammeled, and she was fascinated by its changing seasons and their correspondence to her own inner moods. Although her direct observations were confined to meadows, forests, hills, flowers, and a fairly small range of little creatures, these provided material highly suitable to her personal vision and impressive symbols for her inner conflicts. Unlike the major English and American Romantic poets, her view of nature as beneficent is balanced by a feeling that the essence of nature is baffling, elusive, and perhaps destructive.

Her nature poems divide into those that are chiefly presentations of scenes appreciated for their liveliness and beauty, and those in which aspects of nature are scrutinized for keys to the meaning of the universe and human life. The distinction is somewhat artificial but still useful, for it will encourage consideration of both the deeper significances in the more scenic poems and of the pictorial elements in the more philosophical poems. As we have noted, nature images and metaphors permeate Dickinson's poems on other subjects and some of those poems may be more concerned with nature than at first appears.

"It sifts from Leaden Sieves" (311) shows Dickinson combining metaphor and imagery to create a winter scene of great beauty. The poem does not name the falling snow which it describes, thereby increasing a sense of entranced wonder. The "leaden sieves" that stand for an overcast sky also contribute to the poem's initially somewhat sad mood, a mood that is quickly changed by the addition of images that suggest a healing process. The following five lines show everything in the scene becoming peacefully smooth. With the third stanza, the observer's eyes have dropped from sky, horizon, and distant landscape to neighboring fences and fields. The fence becoming lost in fleeces parallels the image of wool, and the image of "celestial vail" (meaning *veil*) skillfully provides a transition between the two stanzas and brings a heavenly beauty to what had been the dissolution of harvested fields. Perhaps it also implies something blessed about the memorial which it makes to those harvests. The idea of snow providing a monument to the living things of summer adds a gentle irony to the poem, for snow is traditionally a symbol of both death and impermanence. In the last stanza, the observer takes delight in a close-up thing, the queenly appearance of fence posts, and then, in a tone of combined relief and wonder, the poem suggests that the lovely winter scene has really had no external source, but has simply arrived by a kind of inner or outer miracle. Our analysis can provide a basis for further symbolic interpretation of the poem.

An apparently more cheerful scene appears in the popular "I'll tell you how the Sun rose" (318). This poem divides evenly into two metaphorical descriptions – of a sunrise and a sunset on the same day. The speaker assumes the guise of a little girl urgently running with news of nature, delighted with the imaginativeness of her perception and phrasing, and pretending bafflement about the details and meaning of the sunset. The sun's rising is described as if it were donning ribbons, which is paralleled by hills untying their bonnets. The ribbons are thin strips of colored clouds which are common at sunrise, and which, as it gets lighter, might seem to appear in various and changing colors "a ribbon at a time." The news "running like squirrels" creates excitement in the scene, for squirrels do become active when the sun rises. The sound of the bobolinks prompts the speaker to address herself softly, holding in her excitement. At midpoint, the poem skips over the whole day, as if the speaker had remained in a trance. She claims to be unable to describe the sunset. Not surprisingly, the images for the sunset are more metaphorical than those for the sunrise. The entire scene is presented in terms of little school children climbing a stile (steps over a hedge). They go over the horizon into a different field, where a "dominie" (an archaic term for schoolmaster or minister) shepherds them away. The yellow children are the waning shafts of light and the purple stile is the darkening clouds at sunset. Sunset clouds are a traditional symbol of a barred gateway into another mysterious world of space and time, or into heaven. Dickinson has gently domesticated what may be a fearful element in the scene.

In several of her most popular nature portraits, Dickinson focuses on small creatures. Two such poems, "A narrow Fellow in the Grass" (986) and "A Bird came down the Walk" (328), may at first seem quite different in scene and tone, but close scrutiny reveals similarities. In "A narrow Fellow in the Grass" (986), as in "It sifts from Leaden Sieves," Dickinson does not name her subject, probably in order to create a mood of surprise or wonder in the reader, paralleling the speaker's reactions. "A narrow fellow," of course, is a snake. The use of "fellow" for the snake combines a colloquial familiarity with a sense of something presumptuously foreign to the speaker's habitat. The first two stanzas paint a very vivid picture of the smooth movement and semi-invisibility of a snake in deep grass. If one does not meet him (as if by introduction or full vision), one gets the shock of seeing grass divide evenly as a signal of his unseen approach. Surprise is continued by the snake's proceeding in a similarly semi-magical way. After this eight-line introduction, the poem slows down for the next eight lines as the speaker reflects on the snake's preference for cool, moist terrain, where perhaps she ventured when younger, or from which a snake once ventured into territory closer to her. We call Dickinson's speaker "her" despite the curious and significant reference to herself as a boy. Dickinson uses a male persona in a few other poems. Here, she is probably thinking of herself as a boy to stress her desire for the freedom of movement which her society denied to girls. Reflecting now on an earlier encounter with a similar snake, Dickinson describes the snake as a whiplash to emphasize its complete disguise when it lies still, a description that pairs neatly with the snake's concealed comb-like appearance in the second stanza. When she tried to pick up the whiplash and it had disappeared, she apparently was not overly surprised. Her desire to secure the whiplash is a faint echo of the tying of the worm with a string in "In Winter in my Room" (1670).

After the reflective interlude of the middle eight lines, Dickinson makes some general conclusions in the last eight lines. The reference to creatures as being nature's "people" is similar to the personification of "fellow," but it lacks its touch of disdain. She is moved to cordiality by other creatures because they recognize her and, in so doing, they have at least one human quality. But the snake belongs to a distinctly alien order. Even if she is accompanied when she meets one, she always experiences an emotional shock that grips her body to its innermost parts. The famous phrase "zero at the bone" converts a number into a metaphor for frightful and cold nothingness. The snake has come to stand for an evil or aggressive quality in nature – a messenger of fear where she would prefer to greet the familiar, the warm, and the reassuring. However, there seems to be ambivalence in her attitude; her vivid and carefully accurate, though fanciful, observation of the snake implies some admiration for the beauty and wonderful agility of the strange animal. The combination of such homely details and diction as "fellow," "comb," "boggy," "whiplash," and "wrinkled" with such formal terms as "notice," "secure," "transport," and "cordiality" gives the poem a particularly American and Dickinsonian flavor. One cannot imagine a Wordsworth or a Tennyson using anything but consistently formal diction for such description, and the American poets Bryant and Longfellow would have made such a sight an occasion for both a formal description and a positive moral. This poem is both descriptive and philosophical, and it runs counter to the tradition of poems that claim to see good intentions in nature.

The almost equally popular "A Bird came down the Walk" (328) is more cheerful than "A narrow Fellow" and more descriptive, but it also deals with man's alienation from nature. In the snake poem, the speaker is threatened by an emanation of nature. Here, she unsuccessfully tries to cross the barrier between man and nature as it is embodied in a less threatening creature. The first two stanzas show the bird at home in nature, aggressive towards the worm which it eats and politely indifferent to the beetle. The description of the angleworm as being a fellow eaten raw simultaneously humanizes the little creature and places it in a diminutive animal world. The speaker is enjoying her secret spying, which adds to the tension of the scene, a tension that becomes more explicit in the third stanza's description of the bird's frightened uneasiness. Its natural habitat is being invaded, and the speaker appreciates the bird's increased beauty under stress, a stress which is implied by the metaphors of its eyes being like beads and its head being like velvet.

In the fourth stanza, tension is divided between the speaker, who, rather than the bird, now seems to be in danger, and the bird who is about to flee. This device shows the speaker identifying with the bird, a sign of her desire for an intimacy that the bird will reject. The last six lines use metaphors for the bird that counter the humanizing touches of the opening stanzas, and they also counter the somewhat alienated tone of the middle stanza with more aesthetic images of the bird's power, ease, and union with nature. The bird departs into an ocean of air where all of creation is seamless. Probably the ambiguous quality in the speaker's experience is intended to contrast with the atmosphere of relaxed, almost cosmic, unity of these closing lines. Written in primarily iambic rhythm, the poem communicates its uneasy tone partly through its subtle metrical variation, chiefly reversal of accent, and through its cacophonous sounds – all largely in the first three stanzas. In the last two stanzas, the rhythms become smoother and the sounds more euphonious, in imitation of the bird's smooth merging with nature.

Mixed feelings of a different kind are striking in "The Wind begun to knead the Grass" (824), one of the finest of Dickinson's many poems about storms with (and occasionally without) rain. Not until the end of this poem do we realize that the speaker is probably safely inside a house and looking out of a door or a window at a developing storm. The details of the scene are presented in a series of vigorous personifications and metaphors. In the first eight lines, the wind is rising and sweeping across the land. Its force makes some of the grass stand up high and some lie down. The analogy to women kneading and tossing dough creates aesthetic detachment. The description of leaves unhooking themselves and dust scooping itself animates the landscape and conveys a sense of excitement about the release of power. The speaker is excited both by this manifestation of strength and by her safe situation, where no road for escape is needed. The human element enters very briefly with the "quickened wagons" that imply both fear and the vigor of fleeing people. Lightning is a giant bird whose head and toe stand for its jagged sweep (these details are clearer and more consistent in Dickinson's second version of the poem, which accompanies the first version in the *Complete Poems* and in the variorum edition). Birds putting up bars to nests humanizes their actions and parallels the behavior of people. All the images of flight thus far, including the description of the landscape, build up a tension which begins to ease with the description of the drop of giant rain, but the tension is maintained by the repeated "thens" and by the metaphor of hands holding up a dam, until these hands part and the rain comes. This passage creates the feeling of a breathless participation in the scene by the speaker, as if she herself were holding back the torrent. When the released waters "wreck" the sky (it has become a structure paralleling her dwelling), she is safe inside her father's house looking at a tree that has been split by lightning. It seems to please the speaker to see nature as both alien and familiar, wild and domestic. She enjoys watching the release of power in nature and can empathize with it while she remains in the safety of her home. The understatement of the last two lines suggests that she accepts her protected situation as a natural aspect of her life.

The very popular "A Route of Evanescence" (1463) often puzzles readers until they learn that Dickinson referred to it as "My hummingbird." Several critics have been interested in it as a possible revision of the earlier and not very accomplished "Within my Garden, rides a Bird" (500). "A Route of Evanescence" appears to be more purely descriptive than the snake and bird poems which we have discussed, but some readers have found philosophical elements in it. For analysis, the poem can be divided into three parts. The first four lines describe a hummingbird in flight. The first line presents a paradox—the route or path of the hummingbird is made of evanescence because the bird's speed denies its substantiality; bird and route have become identical. In the second line, the bird's whirring wings are a revolving wheel, a more definite image and therefore easier for us to apprehend, even though the bird is still seen as a blur. The third line employs synesthesia—the description of one sense in terms of another. Here the emerald of the bird's back and wings is a resonating sound, probably to give a sense of vibration. The fourth line is close to synesthesia in representing the bird's ruby-colored throat as "a rush of cochineal," a fusion of kinesis and sight. The fifth and sixth lines describe the bird's gathering nectar from the flowers from the blossom's own point of view. The blossoms are personified, and we sense an identification between speaker and flower. In the last two lines, the speaker comments on the whole experience. Tunis, in North Africa, is approximately 8,000 miles from New England. A morning's ride from there would be incredibly swift. The poet is implying by such an accomplishment that the bird is completely at home in nature and serenely confident of its power. These last two lines probably allude to a passage in Shakespeare's *The Tempest* in which a message from Naples to Tunis (a mere 400 miles was huge in the ancient world) could not be expected "unless the sun were post."

In the popular "I taste a liquor never brewed" (214), Emily Dickinson describes an intoxicated unity of self and nature without the alienation that haunts some of her other nature poems. Unlike most of the nature poems that we have discussed, this one describes not a scene but a state of mind. In the first line, the poet shows that the experience is just beginning by her use of the word "taste," which implies a sensation not yet dominant. The grammar of the second line is puzzling. The tankards may be places for real alcohol, or they may be her drinking vessels, in which case the pearl would refer to the preciousness or rarity of the experience. As soon as we read the poem's third and fourth lines, we see that a liquor never brewed must be a spiritual and not a physical substance, and her rejection of what comes from vats on the Rhine, a distant and romantic place, shows her reveling in the superiority of her home surroundings, no matter how small their compass. In the second and third stanzas, she is drunk on the essence of summer days, which seem endless. The formal diction of "inebriate" and "debauchee" light-heartedly spiritualizes the intoxication. Dickinson creates her scene of endless summer in a very few images, the image of "Molten blue" and the relatively simple images of bees, flowers, and butterflies being sufficient. The word "molten" gives us simultaneously the sense of a fluid sky along with a feeling of dissolving into this sky, and it is also a symbol for the spiritual liquor being drunk. This simplification imparts to the speaker's reveling a childlike quality in keeping with the poem's quick transformation of the sensuous into the spiritual. The third stanza suggests that no one can own the things of nature, and that when butterflies have had their fill of nectar, the speaker will go on drinking from nature's spiritual abundance. Her continued drinking indicates her insatiability but may also imply the triumph of her imagination over the decline of summer. In the last stanza, she has ascended into heaven, perhaps by the way of sunbeams, and heavenly angels come to the windows of paradise to see this spiritual drunkard leaning against the sun for rest. For the variorum edition, Thomas Johnson accepted a much different and tamer variant for the last two lines, but he restored the famous sun-tippler in *Complete Poems* and in *Final Harvest*. This poem has been compared to Emerson's "Bacchus," and one critic has suggested that Dickinson is parodying Emerson's poem. The comparison is interesting, but the poems are quite different in tone, the Emerson poem communicating an intense pathos much more reminiscent of Emily Dickinson in her poems which deal with her dark contemplations of the mysteries of the cosmic process.

Emily Dickinson's more philosophical nature poems tend to reflect darker moods than do her more descriptive poems and are often denser and harder to interpret. The nature scenes in these poems often are so deeply internalized in the speaker that a few critics deny the reality of their physical scenes and insist that the poems deal exclusively with states of mind. Our observation of the blending of idea with scene in the nature poems which we have already discussed cautions us against such an extreme view. It is more accurate to say that the philosophical nature poems look outward and inward with equal intensity.

In "What mystery pervades a well!" (1400), nature is seen as a large-scale abstraction. Although it is more expository than most of Dickinson's philosophical nature poems, it still maintains a balance between abstraction, metaphor, and scene. The imagery is centered on a well whose strange and frightening depths the speaker contemplates until her mind moves on to larger vistas of nature and finally, quite probably, to a contemplation of death. In the first two stanzas, we are made aware of the close and familiar aspects of a well and of its mystery. The metaphor of a neighbor from another world contained in a jar typifies Dickinson's combination of the familiar and the mysterious. In the second stanza, the homely lid of glass becomes terrifying when converted into "an abyss's face," one of Dickinson's most brilliant uses of a metaphor to represent an abstraction. The third and fourth stanzas show nature at home with itself, suggested by the grass's and the sedge's familiarity with wells and with the sea. In the last two stanzas, Dickinson grows more abstract and yet she preserves considerable drama through the personification of nature, the actions of those that study it, and the frightening results. She is skeptical about the real knowledge of those who most frequently talk of nature, evidently referring to transcendental philosophers and analytical scientists. Such people are pompous fools because they do not realize that nature's mysteries are ultimately unknowable. If they had ever looked at nature closely they would have become baffled and probably frightened by her and would not so glibly use her name.

The haunted house and the ghost bring up the question of death's relation to nature, which is further explored in the last stanza. There are possibly two different, but not necessarily contradictory, ideas here. Perhaps in the last two lines Dickinson is saying that the more an individual knows about a complicated subject such as nature, paradoxically the less he knows because he becomes aware that there is so much more to know and that there is so much that it is impossible to know. But it is more likely that Dickinson is suggesting that the closer a person comes to death, which is an aspect of nature, the fewer resources he has left to understand it because of waning powers of mind and body. Dickinson implies that to know nature fully is to be dead, which seems to be a more regrettable state than the pitiable state of ignorance.

Turning to Dickinson's more descriptive philosophical poems of nature, we start with the genial and popular "These are the days when Birds come back" (130), written in about 1859, a few years before the full flowering of her genius. The days when birds come back make up Indian summer, an event of great beauty in rural New England. As an early critic of this poem noted, birds do *not* return during Indian summer, and bees continue to gather nectar whenever they can. The scene, however, remains convincing, for we all have witnessed the persistence of some birds in early autumn, and we can understand the speaker's identification with bees, whose supposed skepticism is part of her mood. The poem dramatizes the speaker's unwillingness to see the year die, along with her acceptance of that death and an affirmation of a rebirth in nature. The bird's backward look symbolizes the speaker's yearning for the vanished summer. The sophistries of June are its false arguments that it will last forever – a feeling that Dickinson yields to in "I taste a liquor never brewed." The blue and gold mistake represents bright skies and changing leaves as false signs of persisting vitality.

The third stanza begins a transition with the speaker starting to resist the fraud that she would like to believe in. The seeds of the fourth stanza bear witness (a religious term) that the year's cycle is indeed running down, but these seeds also promise rebirth. The altered air emphasizes the reality of autumn, and the personified timid leaf partly stands for the apprehensive speaker and her fear of mortality. These two stanzas show her beginning to believe in a rebirth despite the atmosphere of decline, and this ambiguity is maintained in the last two stanzas. The supreme moment of Indian summer is called a last communion. The haze describes the literal atmosphere of such a scene and also suggests the speaker's sense of two seasons dissolving into each other and herself dissolving into the scene. These last two stanzas form a prayer in which she is asking to join in what she sees as nature's sacred celebration of the end of summer – she wants to be part of the sad joy of the time. The emblems and consecrated bread and wine are the apparatus of the Christian communion, but the poem presents them as part of the scene: seeds that will flower, and sap that will rise again, although the immortal wine is more an emotional condition in the speaker than an image. If we stress the Christian analogies, we can interpret the poem as an affirmation of conventional immortality, but it is more likely that it celebrates the immortality of the cycle of life while indulging in a bittersweet pathos about the beauty of the season's and life's decline.

Dickinson's novel stanza and rhyme pattern contribute to her effects. Except for the first, the stanzas all employ a rhymed couplet plus a shortened line which rhyme in pairs. The variation in the first stanza is effective; here, the first and third lines use a partial rhyme echoed at the end of the second stanza, and in the second line there is vowel rhyme (assonance) in "resume" and "June." This interlocking parallels the stop-and-go action of the bird's return, the backward look, and the colorful mistake. The metrical and rhyme patterns emphasize the hesitancy and yearning at each stanza's end. "Sophistries of June" and "blue and gold mistake" show Dickinson turning physical phenomena into metaphorical abstractions. The gentle personification of leaves prepares for the conversion of natural elements into religious symbols in the last stanza. We have seen the Dickinson persona in the form of a child in several other poems but never as strikingly. Here, the child guise suggests that the speaker is trying to hold onto faith. In her sterner poems about seasonal change, the childlike stance is absent.

Although "Of Bronze – and Blaze" (290) is not based on seasonal change, it provides material for an interesting contrast to "These are the days." Apparently written only two years after that poem, this one employs a completely different tone in its treatment of human mortality. The pre-variorum editions of Dickinson give the word "daisies" in place of "beetles" in the poem's last line in accordance with a manuscript variant. This grammatically difficult poem begins with a description of the aurora borealis, or northern lights, frequently visible in New England. Only the first two lines, however, present the physical occurrence. The rest of the poem elaborates on its meanings and their significance for the speaker's life. The northern lights are a display of awe-inspiring beauty, and watching them, the speaker is struck by their completely self-contained quality. The third line can mean "it forms an adequate conception of itself or the universe," or "forms" can be read as taking the object "unconcern" in the sixth line, in which case an understood "which" must be inserted before "infects my simple spirit." The sense of the lines is that this beauty in nature shows the sovereign universe to be indifferent to everything except itself or the processes that create it. Dickinson describes its influence on herself as infectious. Its contagious excitement is not proper or healthy for people because it makes them elevate themselves beyond the human sphere. The speaker's strutting on her stem proclaims her lofty pretensions and her revolt from ordinary organic life. She disdains the sustenance of oxygen because she wants to live superior to all human limitations, displaying an arrogance like that which the universe flaunts in these blazing lights.

The splendors mentioned in the second stanza are probably the poet's creations. As "menagerie" (Dickinson is turning this noun into an adjective), her creations have variety and charm but they are severely limited. The northern lights are beyond all competition because they manifest the coldly self-contained power and beauty of the universe itself. The fact that the lights are described as both unconcerned and arrogant suggests that arrogance is a quality which humans feel and project but which the universe does not need. That this show will entertain the centuries means that it will go on forever, while the poet dies and becomes dust. The grass is dishonored because it is nourished by the poet's lowly body. Thoughtless beetles crossing her grave illustrate the unworthiness of her dust and imply that death is extinction. The word "competeless" stresses the inability of the artist to even approximate the magnificence of the general creation.

Unlike "These are the days," this poem shows Emily Dickinson alienated from the natural processes that symbolize immortality. The poem need not, however, be read as wholly pessimistic. The speaker criticizes herself for imitating the arrogance of the cosmos, but she also seems to be reveling in the energy that she acquires from making such an imitation. In the second stanza, she seems to be both affirming the value of her own artistic creations and taking pleasure in the superiority of the universe to herself. On the psychological level, she is perhaps preparing herself for a turn towards conventional religious faith or towards that celebration of the poet's supremacy that we will see in several poems about the poet and artist. These different possibilities suggest the numerous and powerful thrusts of Emily Dickinson's mind in various directions.

In several of Dickinson's best poems, the elevating and the destructive qualities of nature balance one another. Perhaps the best known of these is the widely anthologized "There's a certain Slant of light" (258). As are several of Dickinson's best philosophical poems, this one is also related to a moment of seasonal change. The scene is further along in the year than that of "These are the days," and the poetic artist is more mature (although the poem was written only about two years later). With the exception of its last two lines, this poem presents few difficulties in its word choice or grammar. Nevertheless, it shows so much intensity and strangeness of feeling that when most students first read it, they are usually puzzled.

The physical substance of the scene appears only in the first two lines of its opening stanzas and in its concluding stanzas. The landscape seems to be a meadowland, perhaps with trees and hills, for one gets a sense of expanse and looming objects. On winter afternoons, the sunlight is diminished because the northern hemisphere is inclined away from the sun, making the days shorter and the sun's rays less direct. Also, there is often a cloud cover. The first stanza stresses the heaviness of the atmosphere. Beyond this initial observation, a discussion of the poem should begin with an examination of the parallels and differences among its four stanzas. Their most obvious similarity is the presence of interrelated paradoxes in the first three stanzas, which are echoed by the paradoxical tone of the last stanza.

In the first stanza, cathedral tunes that oppress join a mood of depression to the elevating thought of cathedrals, and in the second stanza, this paradox is concisely suggested by "Heavenly Hurt," which connects bliss with pain. This mixed feeling in the third stanza is called the "Seal Despair," seal referring to the stamped impressure or wax attachment of a king or a government on a document, which guarantees its authenticity, and perhaps referring also to the biblical seals that open to admit the saved into paradise. In the third stanza, "imperial affliction" further reinforces this paradox. This phrase continues the imagery of royalty begun by "seal," and also "affliction" is a typical Bible term for suffering that requires the healing of God.

In the second stanza, "it" refers to the slant of light with its hidden message, but in the third stanza, "it" refers only to that message, which has now become internalized in the speaker. In the last stanza, "it" is once more the slant of light, now perceived as mysterious. The landscape, symbolic of human perception, listens; and shadows, probably symbols of darkened understanding, hold their breath in anticipation of understanding the meaning of the winter light. When the light goes, its going resembles either the fading of consciousness in the eyes of dying persons, or the look in the eyes of personified death itself. Because these last two lines are so condensed, it is difficult to choose between these two interpretations. Although the light seems to symbolize death at the end of the poem, its association with cathedrals in the first stanza modifies this symbolism. The imagery of the opening lines and the tone of the poem as a whole suggest that this strange, pale, and somber light can give to the human spirit a feeling of exultation even while it is portending death.

The second stanza tells us that this winter light inflicts a spiritual wound, and the third stanza explains that this suffering cannot be taught, given consolation, or even explanation. The implication is that such suffering is precious as well as painful. Perhaps it is also implied that the soul belongs to and will find itself most truly in heaven. However, these final stanzas seem to be more concerned with the deepening of human sensibility on earth. Thus, it is likely that the "seal despair" passage is saying that we become aware of our spirituality and experience the beauty of the world most intensely when we realize that mortality creates this spirituality and beauty.

The style of this poem is representative of Dickinson in a meditative mood. The sense impressions employ synesthesia (light and sound are given weight). The "heavenly hurt," "seal despair," and "imperial affliction" turn abstractions for emotions into semi-pictorial metaphors and thereby give a physical feeling to purely internal experiences. The last stanza returns to the physical world but assigns to its personified landscape the feelings of a person who is observing such a scene.

"As imperceptibly as Grief" (1540) is often compared to "There's a certain Slant of light" as another poem in which seasonal change becomes a symbol of inner change. The relationship of inner and outer here, however, is somewhat different. "There's a certain Slant" begins with a moment of arrest that signals the nature and meaning of winter. This poem tells us that summer has passed but insists that this passing occurred so slowly that it did not seem like the betrayal that it really was. The comparison to the slow fading of grief also implies a failure of awareness on the speaker's part. The second and third lines begin a description of a transitional period, and their claim that the speaker felt no betrayal shows that she has had to struggle against such a feeling. The next eight lines create a personified scene of late summer or early autumn. The distilled quiet allows time for contemplation. The "twilight long begun" suggests that the speaker is getting used to the coming season and is aware that change was occurring before she truly noticed it. These lines reinforce the poem's initial description of a slow lapse and also convey the idea that foreknowledge of decline is part of the human condition. The personification of the polite but coldly determined guest who insists on leaving no matter how earnestly she is asked to stay is convincing on the realistic level. On the level of analogy, the courtesy probably corresponds to the restrained beauty of the season, and the cold determination corresponds to the inevitability of the year's cycle.

The movement from identification with sequestered nature to nature as a departing figure communicates the involvement of humans in the seasonal life cycle. The last four lines shift the metaphor and relax the tension. Summer leaves by secret means. The missing wing and keel suggest a mysterious fluidity – greater than that of air or water. Summer escapes into the beautiful, which is a repository of creation that promises to send more beauty into the world. The balanced picture of the departing guest has prepared us for this low-key conclusion.

A similar but more difficult poem is "Further in Summer than the Birds" (1068). This poem's imagery and syntax are very concentrated, and a line-by-line analysis is helpful in understanding it, although Emily Dickinson lends some assistance by describing the poem as "my cricket" in one of her letters. The phrase "further in summer than the birds" indicates that the time of year is late summer when noisy insects proliferate, rather than early summer when bird-song is predominant. The crickets are pathetic in the spectator's eyes because they are small and doomed, unlike the birds who will winter over or go south. Their concealment in the grass concentrates the poet's attention on their song and helps her to consider them "a minor nation." As do Catholics, they celebrate a Mass – an enactment of a sacrifice with a promise of resurrection.

The second stanza continues to stress the insects' invisibility, again with sound replacing sight. An ordinance is the sign of a change in a phase of a religious ritual. There are changes in the crickets' mass, but they are too continuous and subtle to be perceived. The grace which the crickets seek or celebrate is gradual because it is part of the life process that they are rehearsing in their pulsing rhythm. In the seventh line, "pensive custom" is a more definite personification of the insects than the implicit personification of the earlier lines because it suggests a willed rather than an automatic action. This provides for a smooth transition to the enlargement of loneliness, because this idea clearly applies more to the speaker than to the crickets – if it doesn't apply exclusively to her – for the apparently thoughtless crickets have the companionship of their nation, whereas the contemplative speaker seems to be observing them in isolation. She is looking ahead to the loneliness of winter when she will not have even the companionship of nature and its small creatures.

In the word "antiquest," Dickinson invents a comparative form for the adjective "antique" – meaning "most antique." The crickets' mass seems most antique; that is – primeval, ancient, rooted in the very foundation of the world or of nature – at what is for Dickinson the moment of life's greatest intensity, noon. Other poems and passages of her letters reveal that noon often represented for her immortality or perfection. Also the juxtaposition of "noon" and "burning low" in these lines suggests the double nature of autumn; it is a season characterized by the brightness of high noon, but it is also the season where everything is "burning low" or "running down." The "spectral Canticle" is a ghostly religious song. Throughout the first three stanzas, the extensive use of *m*'s and *n*'s emphasizes the drowsiness of the late summer scene; these humming sounds are pensive, and like the crickets' song, they also "typify" repose – sleep and death.

The final stanza, as in other Dickinson poems on similar themes, moves from meditation back towards the physical scene. Its first line says that the grace or beauty of the world remains undiminished. "Furrow on the glow" is one of Dickinson's strangest figures of speech. A furrow is a physical depression or cleavage, usually made by plowing or shoveling earth. The glow is the general beauty of nature. She is creating with her fused image of earth and light a metaphorical picture to repeat the idea that this beauty is undiminished. The Druids were ancient pagan priests and prophets who sometimes practiced human sacrifice. A "druidic difference" would mean that this aspect of nature prophesies a coming magical and mysterious change, but this prospect of change enhances rather than mars nature. Also, there is an implication in these lines that nature and its small creatures are sacrificing themselves so that spring will come again with all of its abundance. Probably the simplest explanation of the "enhancement" is that it is due to our increased awareness of natural beauty, or of life itself, when we reflect on its coming disappearance, an idea which we have found in other Dickinson nature poems.

Despite their relative brevity, Dickinson's philosophical nature poems are often quite rich in meaning and connotation, and they can be re-read and re-experienced from many angles. This is certainly true for one of the shortest of her nature poems, "Presentiment – is that long Shadow – on the lawn" (764). Although there are personifications in this poem, the scene is real and resembles those in Dickinson's poems about seasonal change. In the long and slow-moving first line, the speaker is in a contemplative mood and sees the shadow of night move across a lawn – usually a place of domestic familiarity and comfort. Thought and experience seem to have occurred to her simultaneously. The formal word "indicative" and the generalized image of setting suns suggest the universality of her fear of the coming darkness and implicitly link darkness with death. The second two lines personify both the shadow of night and the grass. The darkness announces its approach with a formal detachment that resembles that of the quest in "As imperceptibly as Grief." The startled grass symbolizes the speaker's inner self as the darkness looms up suddenly. The tone of these lines is similar to the mood suggested by the listening landscape in "There's a certain Slant." The conclusion of the poem is deliberately abrupt, creating a dramatic tension between it and the slow contemplation of the first two lines. The speaker seems to be displaying cool resolve in the face of her shock, but we know nothing of the content of her thoughts. As do most of Dickinson's philosophical nature poems, this one shows the poet confronting mystery and fright with a combination of detachment and involvement.

Poetry, Art, and Imagination

A close examination of Emily Dickinson's letters and poems reveals many of her ideas, however brief, about poetry and on art in
general, although most of her comments on art seem to apply chiefly to poetry. Many of her poems about poetic art are cast in
allegorical terms that require guesswork and parallels from other of
her poems for their interpretation. Although we are mostly concerned with the meaning and value of these poems, it is interesting
and useful to note that the views which they express about
aesthetics can fit into many significant theories about literature.
For example, if one uses M. H. Abrams's convenient four-fold division of theories of literature: imitative (the poet re-creates reality);
expressive (the poet expresses his inner feelings); pragmatic or af-
fective (the poet seeks to move his audience); objective (the poet
tries to construct self-contained works of art) — one finds comments
and poems by Emily Dickinson that support all of these theories.
She sees poems as artifacts giving permanence to the fading world
and the mortal poet. She sees the poet achieving relief, personal
identity, and communication through poetry. She sees the poet as a
seer, yet she despairs of the poet's power to capture the final
mysteries. She sees poetry as being able to open new visions and
the heart of its hearers to perspectives and ideas which they otherwise miss. She distinguishes between the false and the genuine in
poetry, and she chides herself for sometimes failing to make the
distinction in her own work. Perhaps her chief emphasis is on the
poet's building a world and gaining relief from his expressions, but
it is easiest to discuss her relevant poems by moving from those
treating the poet's relationship to audience and world to those
treating the poet's inner world.

A number of Emily Dickinson's poems about poetry relating the
poet to an audience probably have their genesis in her own frustrations and uncertainties about the publication of her own work. "This is
my letter to the World" (441), written about 1862, the year of Emily
Dickinson's greatest productivity, looks forward to the destiny of her
poems after her death. The world that never wrote to her is her whole
potential audience, or perhaps centrally its literary guardians, who
will not recognize her talent or aspirations. She gives nature credit for
her art and material in a half-apologetic manner, as if she were merely
the carrier of nature's message. The fact that this message is com

mitted to people who will come after her transfers the precariousness of her achievement to its future observers, as if they were somehow responsible for its neglect while she was alive. The plea that she be judged tenderly for nature's sake combines an insistence on imitation of nature as the basis of her art with a special plea for tenderness towards her own fragility or sensitivity; but poetry should be judged by how well the poet achieves his or her intention and not by the poem alone, as Emily Dickinson surely knew. This particular poem's generalization about her isolation – and its apologetic tone – tend towards the sentimental, but one can detect some desperation underneath the softness.

"If I shouldn't be alive" (182), an earlier poem than "This is my letter," is a firmer and more powerful statement of a similar idea, thematically richer and with a different twist. Here, the poet-speaker anticipates being cut off from the splendid presence of nature by death. The time of robins is the spring, a season of joyous rebirth, and the robin-as-singer is a fellow poet. The robin's red cravat is a witty, half-personifying touch, giving the bird something of that nervy artifice that sustained Dickinson. The memorial crumb serves to remind us of the poet's own slim spiritual nourishment by those who might have recognized and sustained her, as well as of the small needs of robins. Although the second stanza continues the conditional mood, it moves more decisively into the time when the poet will be dead; hence, it anticipates those brilliant later poems in which Emily Dickinson's speaker is dying or speaks from beyond the grave. The speaker's being fast asleep combines a note of relief with sadness at the loss of all feeling, leaving a striking shock effect for the climactic last two lines. If she is fast asleep, her efforts to speak through that sleep show the spirit at war with death – rebellious against the arrest of the voice with which she brought nature to expression and drew close to it. The image of the granite lip combines the sense of body as mere earth with body as the energy of life. Possibly, granite also suggests the potential power of her expression or even the strength of her unrecognized poems. The parallels to other Emily Dickinson poems about robins as poets, effortful expression as poetry, and poetry as a challenge to death support this interpretation. The consistency, rich suggestiveness, and emotional complexity of this poem mark it as a superior effort in what may, on a first reading, seem to be merely a casual vein.

"Essential Oils – are wrung" (675) is an equally personal but more allegorical comment on poems as a personal challenge to death. It is the same length as "This is my letter" and "If I shouldn't be alive," but its highly compressed images and action make it a richer poem. The central symbol here is attar (perfume) of roses, expanded to refer to some undefined essence of rose that will lie in a lady's drawer after her death. Surely this image represents Emily Dickinson's poems accumulating in her drawers, as they quite literally did, and finding an audience after her death, as they fortunately did. The wringing of the rose – "expressed" means pressed out or squeezed – combines the creative force of nature as represented by the sun, with the special suffering that sensitive and artistic souls undergo. The first stanza emphasizes creative suffering, and the second stanza emphasizes its marvelous result, but both stanzas combine the sense of suffering and creation. The general *rose* may represent ordinary nature or ordinary humanity, or perhaps merely the idea of natural beauty as opposed to its essence. The marvelous generality of this reference leads us gently but firmly from the attar of roses as an allegorical symbol to all beauty as a symbol of accomplishment. The poem is chiefly allegorical, therefore, but this transition and the stress on the dead lady give it a strange combination of allegorical mystery and concrete reality. The reference to decay reminds us of the physical fate of all things natural – that is, here she evokes a decay challenged by art. The essence of roses – the art as poetry that the lady has created out of nature through effort and suffering – makes nature *bloom* again, or live even more *vividly*, for those who read the poems. The lady lying in ceaseless rosemary may, at first, suggest a contrast between her dead body and the nature that continues around her, but when we recall that rosemary is the flower of remembrance and was often placed in coffins ("There's rosemary, that's for remembrance – pray you, love, remember," says Shakespeare's Ophelia, suggesting even more connotations for Emily Dickinson's line), we may see this phrase as suggesting a special immortality for the lady poet. Although the stress here is on creation through suffering, an aura of triumph and assurance permeates the poem.

"I died for Beauty – but was scarce" (449) should remind us that Emily Dickinson said that John Keats was one of her favorite poets, and it is likely that the poem is partly a simplification and variation on the theme, or at least echoes the conclusion, of his "Ode on a Grecian Urn": "Beauty is truth, truth beauty – that is all/ Ye know on earth, and all ye need to know." The poem's speaker looks back from death to life and laments the cessation of speech – quite probably representing poetic communication. Here, however, rather than our finding a wistful, desperate, or self-assured struggle for posthumous expression, we discover a dignified and almost peaceful resignation. The emphasis here on beauty, truth, and lips correlates to themes about poetry elsewhere in Emily Dickinson, just as the covering up of names on tombstones correlates to her concerns about surviving because of the immortality of her poems. The strangely abrupt use of "adjusted" for the dead suggests a struggle against and a resignation to death. The mutual tenderness of the two buried figures shows lonely souls longing for company, and the use of "failed" for the more normal "died" suggests that the defeat of their art and thought contributed to their deaths, which we are to see as sacrifices. These terms also reflect Emily Dickinson's sense that the novel authenticity of her poems kept people from appreciating them. The mind-teasing problem of equating truth and beauty is perhaps as great in Emily Dickinson's poetry as it is in Keats's poem. One simple interpretation would be that accuracy, penetration, and ordering of vision, at least for the artist, create beauty, and that such efforts are painful almost to the point of self-sacrifice. The kinsmen in the last stanza seem comfortable and cheered by each other, though still separated, but the stilling of their lips by moss and the covering of their names suggest Emily Dickinson's feelings that her struggles for beauty and truth were unavailing in their accessibility – if not in their quality. Nevertheless, the resignation of the poem maintains a fine dignity, and the poem as a whole creates a charming variation on Emily Dickinson's treatments of voices from beyond death and of survival through poetry. Of course, this poem need not be interpreted as a comment on Emily Dickinson's situation as a poet. One can read it merely as a fantasy about the light which death throws on the life struggles of sensitive souls and on the question of their rewards for their struggles, but correlation with other poems supports our interpretation and enriches the suggestiveness of the details.

"Publication – is the Auction" (709) is Emily Dickinson's best-known statement of her feelings about publication, but the poem should be read as a partial and complicated version of her attitudes. The unusual stress on publication as auction (rather than mere sale) may reflect resentment that poets must compete by adjusting their gifts and vision to public taste to earn profitable attention. Poverty would justify such a shaping of skills for the market, but that would strain the poet's integrity. This interpretation, however, may be excessively biographical because of its stress on Emily Dickinson's need for artistic independence, but it is also possible that she was chiefly rationalizing her fear of seeking a public and attributing a white innocence to the seclusion which her fears compelled, or it may be that she is only emphasizing the unworldly purity of art. The poet's garret stands for a worldly poverty which she never experienced, but it does accurately symbolize her isolation. The idea of not investing purity continues the economic metaphor and gives the poem something of a snobbish tone. The two "hims" of the third stanza may refer to God and the poet *or* they may refer to the poet in two guises – as an inspired person and as a craftsman. (It is possible that the poet here is analogous to God becoming man.) The last six lines, switching to a scornful second person, suggest that the poet as human spirit is even more precious than the beauty of nature or the words of God and that reducing his words to a commercial level is blasphemy. The insistent and somewhat wooden trochaic rhythm of the poem enhances and enriches its scorn and determination, but it also communicates some uncertainty about the viewpoint, as if Emily Dickinson were protesting too much. Nevertheless, the curiously mixed diction of the poem, combining commercial, religious, and aesthetic terms gives dignified pride to its anger.

When Emily Dickinson writes about the relationship of poet and audience more distinctly from the viewpoint of the living and with the poet's elevated status in mind, her assertions tend to be less ambiguous, her tone either reverent or triumphant, and her eyes almost equally on what the poet communicates as on the fact of communication. Such poems include "This was a Poet – It is That" (448), "I reckon – when I count at all" (569), and "A Word made Flesh is seldom" (1651). "This was a Poet – It is That" (448), an almost explosively joyous poem, probably celebrates the triumph of some other poet, the speaker basking in reflected glory. The poem combines an analysis of the poet's methods, her visionary power, and her achievement of permanence. The amazing sense and "attar so immense" stress how novelty and compressed expression give new significance to transient beauty and thereby create both envy and surprise about one's own limited vision. The idea that poetry helps us see the familiar freshly by presenting it strangely or with novelty is at least as old as Aristotle's *Poetics*. The third stanza stresses the pictorial quality of poems, as one might expect from an image-maker like Dickinson – no matter how generalized her own picturing. The somewhat puzzling notion that the poet entitles others to poverty may be an ironic pun on "entitling," as giving others a low status, but more likely it means that they can endure their own poverty because they can *borrow* the poet's riches, although both meanings may be intended. The last stanza seems to refer back to the poet a little cryptically and not to those who suffer poverty. The poet's portion is so deep and permanent that he is unconscious of it and will feel no resentment about how much others take from him. Of course, poets are usually pleased and not even unconsciously resentful at lending their vision, so one assumes that Emily Dickinson's overstatement is designed to suggest some strangely personal apprehension about feeding on the spirit of poets – possibly a serious or playful concern with an emotional parasitism in herself, or even in those who will not recognize her ability.

"I reckon – when I count at all" (569) echoes themes from "This was a Poet" but is even more extravagant. Here, the subject is poets in general, who head her list of precious things – before nature and heaven. She then decides that since the work of poets includes nature and heaven, she can dispense with them. Poets are *all* – insofar as their work contains the body of nature and heaven and, by implication, all of experience. Unlike "natural" summers, the summers of poets do not fade, and their suns are brighter than the sun itself. So far, interpretation is easy; in contrast, the last five lines of this poem are more condensed and difficult. The "further heaven" probably means the heaven beyond life – as opposed to the earthly one that poets create or capture. The line "Be Beautiful as they prepare" probably means turning out to be as beautiful as the one that poets create for their worshippers (readers). The last two lines would then mean that it is impossible to imagine a real heaven that could match the heaven that poets have already given us. Emily Dickinson here gives the poet or the poetic imagination a status greater than God's. This extravagance can be attributed to her need for reassurance about the richness of her own narrow living space or of her own creations, or a combination of the two. An equally extravagant poem in which the poet is made superior to God is "This is a Blossom of the Brain" (945); here, poetry is given traits like Emily Dickinson's own shyness, the vitality of nature, and the promise of reproducing its own kind. The mystery of the poetic process and the rare recognition given to it echo Emily Dickinson's feelings about her neglect and isolation as a poet and imply that poets receive more than enough compensation for this neglect by the world. More playful and perhaps less desperate than "I reckon – when I count," this poem may be taken as a deliberate extravaganza or a serious assertion of Emily Dickinson's feelings about art as a religion and her participation in it.

In "A Word made Flesh is seldom" (1651), a Bible text is woven into another assertion of the poet's godlike nature. Here, the first stanza seems to imply that the Christ of the Bible is difficult to know but that something like Him is more available elsewhere and that the private act of securing it gives us joy suitable to our personal identities. That something else seems to be the *word* as spoken by the whole-spirited poet, which is as immortal as God. The speaking of this word seems to satisfy both speaker and audience. If God could dwell among us as flesh, his condescension would need to be extraordinary to match that of the poet. This poem exists only in a transcript, and its original punctuation is perhaps distorted, for it seems to require a question mark at the end, which would make it imply that language brings spirit into flesh more than Christ did.

In several poems, Emily Dickinson stresses the inner world of poetry as the source of joy, identity, and growth. One of the best of these poems is "I dwell in Possibility" (657), perhaps not immediately recognizable as a poem about poetry. Although possibility might refer to an openness to all experience, the contrast of this dwelling place with prose, the emphasis on an interior world which shuts out ordinary visitors so it may welcome others, and the idea of a captured and concentrated paradise virtually guarantees that the subject is the poetic imagination transforming the world and creating objects of satisfaction to the speaker. The windows and doors allow everything the poet needs to enter, while holding out the eyes and presence of intruders. Gambrels, which are slanting roof cones, are transferred from this house of the imagination to the house of the sky, which represents nature or the universe, suggesting the mergence of the poet's inner and outer worlds. The second stanza shows the speaker having the best of both worlds without suffering exposure, which well suits the assured and almost arrogant tone. Once exclusions are firmly established, the tone relaxes, and the slight harshness of the first two stanzas gives over to tenderness in the last stanza, where the parallelism of visitors and occupation allows a secure relaxation. The tender paradox of a wide spread to narrow hands welcomes the paradise of nature and imagination into the poet's spirit and work and emphasizes how greatness of spirit makes a small space infinitely large. A remarkable example of Emily Dickinson's fusion of the concrete with the abstract, and the large with the small, this poem also bears the peculiar signature of her pride in withdrawal, though its boastfulness does not identify the poet with God, as in the two poems just discussed.

A similar but less boastful poem is the very beautiful but rarely anthologized "Alone, I cannot be" (298), where the emphasis is entirely on the arrival of visionary messengers to a self that does not seem to need to ward off intrusions. The fact that these visitors are "recordless" associates the poem with the evanescence of poetry more than with its permanence, as does another interesting variant on the theme of imagination capturing reality, the brilliant but also infrequently anthologized "The Tint I cannot take—is best" (627), which shows some familiar traits of Emily Dickinson's view of the poetic imagination but also severely reverses some of them. Here, the emphasis is on the impossibility of art's capturing the essence of precious experience, especially of nature and of spiritual triumphs. The poem echoes the fleeing grandeur of such experiences but implies that unsuccessful attempts to capture them create something of their preciousness. Rather than asserting that heaven will scarcely equal these experiences or the expression of them, as in "I reckon—when I count at all," this poem's conclusion insists that only beyond death will we capture or experience them in all their essence. Still, the arrogance assigned to the dying attributes greatness of soul to the imaginative person. This poem may have a repressed note of anger, perhaps the other side of the inflated joy with which Emily Dickinson often treats the poet's recreation of his world.

Poetic creation is also viewed sadly in "The Missing All—prevented Me" (985), one of those poems whose subject seems quite indeterminate. Perhaps "the missing all" is a beloved person, a solid religious faith, an acceptable society, or a high status in the social world. In any case, its absence turns the poet's head downward to total concentration on her work—surely her poems. The ironic comments on such unlikely things as the world tearing loose or the sun going out emphasize the scope of her loss and the importance of the effort which she makes to compensate for it. The pretended indifference to the world expressed in the conclusion makes the poetic process all-important but also somehow tragic. The world created by the imagination is not characterized here – as in "I dwell in Possibility" and other poems – and the poem ends with a regretful grandeur.

Although many of the poems discussed here comment on the poet's craft, other poems make it their central subject. "We play at Paste" (320) can be viewed as a comment on spiritual or personal growth, but it is probably chiefly concerned with the growth of a poet's craftsmanship. The poem provides a fine illustration of the allegorical method in a short poem. "Paste" refers to artificial jewelry. Adults do not play with or at the process of making artificial jewelry as a preparation for making real jewelry, nor do they usually regard themselves with scorn when they look back at artificial playthings and adornments. The scene as presented and the strong emotions associated with it are not realistic as given. Thus the paste, the real pearl, and the maker's hands are not ordinary symbols. Rather, they are allegorical symbols (or images or emblems). If the speaker, distancing herself slightly and making herself one of a group by the use of "we," drops an artificial – that is, inauthentic – creation and judges herself ill for making it, objects of art – poems for Emily Dickinson – seem the most likely subject. In the second stanza, she gains the equilibrium of maturity and looks back to see that her earlier creations prepared her for the later and more genuine ones. "New hands" emphasizes the growth of creative skill and perhaps extends the change from artistry to the whole person. The emphasis on tactics, and several sound effects in the second stanza, especially the echoing hard k sounds, again emphasize the effort and precision of craftsmanship. (Alliteration is particularly effective in the first stanza.) This emphasis gives the poem a feeling of crisp restraint, almost an amused detachment, quite unlike the exaltation in poems that celebrate the poet as visionary.

Poems somewhat more specific about the poet's tactics include "Tell all the Truth but tell it slant" (1129), "The thought beneath so slight a film" (210), and "A Spider sewed at Night" (1138), but they tend to be more superficial and less developed, however immediately charming. "Tell all the Truth but tell it slant" (1129) immediately reminds us of all the indirections in Emily Dickinson's poems: her condensations, vague references, allegorical puzzles, and perhaps even her slant rhymes. The idea of artistic success lying in circuit – that is, in complication and suggestiveness – goes well with the stress on amazing sense and jarring paradoxes which we have seen her express elsewhere. But the notion that truth is too much for our infirm delight is puzzling. On the very personal level for Emily Dickinson's mind, "infirm delight" would correspond to her fear of experience and her preference for anticipation over fulfillment. For her, truth's surprise had to remain in the world of imagination. However, superb surprise sounds more delightful than frightening. Lightning indeed is a threat because of its physical danger, and its accompanying thunder is scary, but it isn't clear how dazzling truth can blind us – unless it is the deepest of spiritual truths. We can, however, simplify these lines to mean that raw experience needs artistic elaboration to give it depth and to enable us to contemplate it. The contemplation theme is reasonably convincing but the poem coheres poorly and uses an awed and apologetic tone to cajole us into disregarding its faults. A similar idea is more lucid in the epigrammatic "The thought beneath so slight a film" (210) because here the idea of obscurity is connected to the necessity of great effort for good artistic perception, which links this poem to her praise for "amazing sense" and makes her shyness before the beautiful but frightening mountains symbolic of universal experiences.

In "A Spider sewed at Night" (1138), Emily Dickinson seems to delight in the spider's isolation, determination, and structural success. The short-line rhyming triplets imitate the spider's almost automatic thrusts. The poem says that no one quite knows what the spider is making, but his own knowledge satisfies him. He has built so well that his structures appear permanent. But the poem is strangely open-ended. Without the wistfulness or apology of other poems on art, and with a more distanced boastfulness, this poem leaves the possibility that the spider's web will be quickly swept away. If so, his triumph was entirely in his own mind, and we know nothing of its ultimate significance. Perhaps the spider's constructive process is an analogue for Emily Dickinson's own power as a poet, which promises a kind of permanence which the spider can't achieve. The "ruff of dame" could be a mere decoration for Emily Dickinson herself, and the "shroud of gnome" could refer to Emily Dickinson's signing herself "your gnome" to Higginson – possibly as an answer to his complaints about her gnomic (condensed to the point of obscurity) expression. Such negative connotations would stand in opposition to the poem's assertations about trying to build something immortal. Whatever ironies this poem contains may have been unconscious or slyly intended. It is a fine example of how an Emily Dickinson poem that is lucid on the surface can be looked at from various angles and given nuances or even about-faces of interpretation.

A few other poems on art and poetry deserve brief treatment here. In "I cannot dance upon my Toes" (326), ballet seems to be a metaphor for poetry. Her poor training stands for her unconventional expression, her inability to follow established forms, and her acknowledgment that she cannot express what she wants contradicts the exuberance of other poems and matches the sense of limitation in yet others. Here, the full house of her spirit doesn't seem to display the fairest visitors, but that is probably because an insensitive audience wants a flashy performance. She probably wrote this poem as a secret reply to Higginson's complaints about the awkwardness of her poems. In "It dropped so low – in my Regard" (747), Emily Dickinson is probably echoing themes of "We play at Paste." From what seems an even more mature perspective, she now looks at an earlier creation and criticizes herself for not seeing how unworthy of her best it was. "To hear an Oriole sing" (526) may be chiefly about problems of perception, but it can also be interpreted as a comment on poetry in which Emily Dickinson takes an outside perspective on the innerness of man's response to successful art. The commonness or divinity of the singing depends on the sensitivity of the audience. Reference to the tune's being in the tree may be a covert comment on the conventions of art as opposed to the force of the inspired poet. Perhaps Emily Dickinson is revolting against the dead ear of someone who found her singing flat. In "I would not paint – a picture" (505), Emily Dickinson pretends that her delight in art is more that of an observer than a creator, but as an observer she is filled with life by poetry and art. Perhaps it substitutes differently for the missing all. But as she concludes by pretending to reject her role as poet, she reveals that, for her, the creation and the enjoyment of poetry are fused, or it may be that she merely – for the time being – wishes that the joy of creation could match and merge with the joy of appreciation.

Friendship, Love, and Society

In an enigmatic four-line poem beginning "That Love is all there is" (1765), Emily Dickinson implies that love is impossible to define and that it transcends the need for definition. She seems to be suggesting that we can recognize love either because it fits our souls perfectly or because we can endure the suffering which it brings. She does not present these alternatives; rather, her lines make these alternate interpretations possible. Such ambiguity permeates her love poems, in which fulfillment is often accompanied by loss. With the exception of the Master letters, whose intended recipient we cannot identify, and her later letters to Judge Otis P. Lord, we have nothing by Dickinson which we could call love letters. However, her early correspondence with Susan Gilbert reveals an awareness that the fulfillment of love might be disappointing. Later in life, Emily Dickinson wrote to Samuel Bowles: "My Friends are my 'estate,' " and still later she declared that letters feel to her like immortality because they contain the mind "without corporeal friend." These statements reinforce our sense that perhaps she preferred an imagined consummation of love to any physical reality, and that she sometimes treasured friendship held at a distance more than the actual presence of friends. However, such psychological speculation should be used carefully in interpreting her poems.

There is a blend of love and friendship in a few of Dickinson's poems. Many of her elegies for family members and friends express love and yet do not lament lost loves. Several poems which are addressed to girlfriends have a romantic tinge, but these are not very good. However, there are some poems about dear people who seem to be regarded more as beloved friends than as objects of romantic ardor. In Dickinson's love poems proper, it is possible to distinguish between romantically passionate poems and poems in which there is a curious physical detachment. In this second type, the beloved person sometimes seems so exalted that it is difficult for the reader to see the beloved as an object of desire to the poem's speaker. But the bulk of Dickinson's love poems are certainly not cold, detached, and ethereal. Circumstances and fears may have kept her from physical fulfillment, but the images and actions of many of her love poems are determinedly passionate.

Three popular Dickinson poems about lost friends are similar in length and style. These are "My life closed twice before its close" (1732), "I never lost as much but twice" (49), and "Elysium is as far as to" (1760). Like the first two of Dickinson's poems about poetry that we examined in the preceding section, the first two of these poems are petulant and urgent in tone. "My life closed twice" is less colloquial and concrete than the other two, but equally witty. This poem exists only in a transcript, so we have no idea when it was written. Although heaven and hell are mentioned, and although some critics see the parting as deaths, the parting is probably not the result of death. Probably the subject is the departure of dear friends who are expected to be long lost or forever absent. The reference to life's closing shows Dickinson's turning a statement about a death-like feeling into a metaphor. Something closing before the final close suggests both an overwhelming extinction of the senses and a general collapse, as if the speaker could feel nothing but her ecstasy and grief. She seems to be folding up like a flower. The immortality that may reveal another experience as inexpressible as these two emotions lies beyond death. Life can bring to her no more profound an experience, and her tone is exultant at having encountered something ultimate in life. The description of parting as being both "heaven" and "hell" is brilliantly witty; parting increases the value of the departing person because parting makes us suffer terribly. The idea that suffering and friendship produce an experience almost more rewarding than we can hope to find in heaven parallels Dickinson's celebration of art.

"I never lost as much but twice" (49) is a fine example of Dickinson's jocular blasphemy combined with a quite serious theme. We could place this poem under the headings of death and religion as easily as under friendship. The fact that earlier losses were *in* (literally *to*) the sod surely refers to the death of friends. The contrast of such losses to a present loss by the use of "but . . . that" indicates that this loss is not to death, but it is just as bad and perhaps harder to explain and accept. The descending angels must have brought new friends. The reference to these friends as "store" suggests that they are a treasure and prepares us for the outburst against God as being both a burglar and a banker. The witty placing of "Father!" after these terms strengthens the accusation that God is playing by unfair rules, and the last line shows an abrupt and stubborn resentment against God's cheating. The manuscript of this poem can be dated at about 1858, a number of years after the deaths of Leonard Humphrey and

Benjamin Newton, and yet it is possible that Dickinson is looking back at their deaths and comparing them to the present departure or faithlessness of a friend or a beloved man.

"Elysium is as far as to" (1760), evidently written quite late in Dickinson's life, is a more general poem than the two just discussed, but, rather curiously, it has a stronger sense of physical scene and of the presence of people than either of them. It is true that neither a specific room nor people are described, and that the room may be a symbol of a condition of life, but possibly the very generality of the situation has allowed Dickinson to create more of a scene than she usually attempts. This poem is more complicated than it may at first appear, and it echoes themes from "My life closed twice." "Elysium" is a Latin word for *heaven*. The heaven described is a state of emotional elevation resulting from anticipation of a friend's achieving great happiness, a happiness intensified by the risk of doom. The fortitude of soul may belong to the speaker of the poem as well as to the friend. If this is true, Dickinson is being made happy both by her admiration of her friend's fortitude and by the joy of sharing such endurance with her friend. Similarly, the anticipated arrival may refer to the friend's awaiting his or her fate, or to the speaker's awaiting the arrival and the fate of the friend. The fine restraint of the poem's conclusion, which reinforces the sense of a hushed atmosphere, implies a favorable outcome for the situation, but it is difficult to tell if it directs our attention more to the friend or to the speaker. The combination of such Latinate terms as *Elysium* and *fortitude* with such Anglo-Saxon words as *doom* and *door*, a striking trait of Dickinson's style, adds to the forcefulness and verbal music of this poem.

Fears of love that Emily Dickinson may have felt do not make her much different from the rest of us. Exactly what combination of character and circumstances kept her from a romantic union we will never know. Many of her poems relating to passion and love reflect intense anxiety, but we should not stress their possible abnormality any further than the clarification of these poems requires. This allows us to recognize the unusual in her feelings and possible experiences while still being able to relate them to our own feelings. First, we will consider her poems that are burdened with anxiety, next go on to those in which anxiety is mixed with renunciation, and finally look at those in which the choice of love creates some kind of spiritual union or faith, either on earth or in heaven. But we should remember that these categories often overlap.

"In Winter in my Room" (1670) is surely Dickinson's most explicit treatment of her fear and mixed feelings about love and sex – if we dare to call a poem so purely symbolic a fantasy explicit. The poem exists only in a transcript, and so it cannot be assigned even approximately to a period of Dickinson's life, but it very possibly is a product of her earlier mature years, her early thirties. There do not seem to be reasonable alternatives to the view that the worm-turned-snake is the male sexual organ moving toward a state of excitement and making a claim on the sexuality and life of the speaker. Psychoanalytic theory and speculation about the sexual knowledge of reclusive virgins are no more helpful than is common sense in making this interpretation. Traditionally, snakes are symbols of evil invading an Eden, and snakes in Emily Dickinson's poems sometimes represent a puzzling fearfulness in nature, just as Eden often represents a pure innocence which might be spoiled by the intrusion of a lover. Such symbolism does not contradict the sexual symbolism. Rather, viewing the snake as a symbol of evil, in addition to seeing it as a sexual symbol, helps us to see how ambivalent is the speaker's attitude toward the snake – to see how she relates to it with a mixture of feelings, with mingled fear, attraction, and revulsion. In the first stanza, the speaker appears almost childlike, and the worm-snake is a minor threat that she can control. In the second stanza, the creature appears in a changed and terrifying guise. The transformation seems unexpected, but the snake bears a sign (the old string) that he is the creature that she once tried to control. In the third stanza, she admits to the fear and insincerity that make her call the snake "fair." But her attraction cannot be denied. The statement that the snake fathomed her thoughts implies admiration for its power, and the description of its rhythmic movements reveals more admiration than repulsion. The rhythmic projection of the snake may refer even to the speaker's mental processes, as well as to the snake's actual motion. The last stanza clearly distinguishes between her two encounters with the worm-snake. At the second meeting, she gives no thought to controlling or pacifying him; she runs until she evades him, but the fact that she had hoped to hold him off by her staring somehow mutes the terror, possibly by implying an unconscious recognition of what the snake stands for and of how valid are its claims. It is difficult to say just why the concluding statement, "this was a dream," seems essential to the poem. Without it, we would easily recognize the fantasy element. Certainly the next-to-the-last line – "I set me down" – is too unassertive for a conclusion. Possibly the last line is both an acknowledgment of the unconscious source of the fantasy and an insistence on its being taken very seriously. Perhaps Dickinson is saying here that dreams can't lie.

The much debated poem "I started Early – Took my Dog" (520) has been more popular than "In Winter in my Room." Many critics take it to be about death or about threatening nature, but we prefer to side with those who think it is about fearful anticipations of love or passion. The coy tone of the poet suggests that she may be taking refuge from a symbolic experience involving combined sexual attraction and threat by adopting a child-like attitude. In the first two stanzas, the speaker visits the sea of experience, accompanied by her protective dog. Dogs in Dickinson's poems are often symbols of the self, partly stemming from her many years of companionship with her setter, Carlo. The mermaids in their mysterious beauty may symbolize the repression of the speaker's femininity, in which case the more helpful frigates may represent an urge to accept herself as she is. The speaker's calling herself "Mouse" reveals her timidity. In the third stanza, the threatening sea merges with the threat of a man who may be able to move her emotionally and, hence, prepares her for flight. The climbing of the sea up over her protective clothing (apron, belt, and bodice are particularly domestic) becomes almost explicitly sexual when linked with the image of dew being eaten. A drop of dew which becomes part of the sea would lose its identity. This image recalls images of pleasurable engulfment in other Dickinson poems, but here it is clearly threatening. The speaker flees and the man-sea pursues. Silver heel and shoe filled with pearl add aesthetic charm to the sexual threat. The last stanza shows the pursuing sea-lover disregarding the social surroundings. The town is probably a symbol of the social conventions that reinforced Dickinson's own timidity and gave her something to fall back on when she was overwhelmed by fears. The mighty look of the sea resembles the explicitly acknowledged power of the snake in "In Winter in my Room"; and, as in that poem, this one ends with a kind of stand-off, as if the threatening world of love and passion were recognized by the poet and carefully distanced. As we have noted, other interpretations of this poem are quite arguable, partly because the tone of the poem is so ambivalent. But the mixture of fear and attraction with a defensive playfulness seems to support our view. The poem is built with great care, but its artifice may make its effect less powerful and revealing than the effect obtained from the starker symbolism of "In Winter in my Room."

Dickinson's poems about the renunciation of a proffered love tempt readers and critics to seek biographical interpretations. Many early critics took these poems too literally; they assumed them to be reports of scenes in which Emily Dickinson refused the love offers of a married man, while offering him assurances of her peculiar faith and her hope for reunion after death. Such interpretations probably do not reflect the reality behind these poems. In all likelihood the poems present fantasies which would have emotionally satisfied Dickinson more than her actual lonely renunciation did. These fantasies provide dramatic plots for cathartic poems.

"I cannot live with You" (640) is probably her most popular poem of this kind. This painful and tense poem is grammatically difficult and deserves more space than we can give it. Careful study of its images, progression, and grammar would be a valuable exercise in understanding Dickinson's poetic techniques. The speaker addresses a beloved man from whom she is permanently separated in life. To live with him would be life, she says, implying that she is dead without him. Paradoxically, the only life together possible for them will be when they are in the grave. Two stanzas representing the dead as broken chinaware poignantly and reluctantly praise death over the apparent wholeness of life. In the third stanza, the speaker imagines death scenes in which she would prefer to comfort her dying lover rather than to die with him. She is also reluctant to die with him because that would give her the horrible shock of seeing her lover eclipse Jesus and dim heaven itself. The lover is like God, and love is superior to heaven (just as Dickinson can find the artist's heaven superior to God's). For two stanzas, beginning with "They'd judge Us–How," the speaker's attention moves to the unconventional nature of her love. People, perhaps representing God, would condemn the lovers for breaking some social or ethical tradition. Perhaps the lover is married, a minister, or both, or perhaps the service of heaven is a more general stewardship. The speaker's desperation now threatens the poem's coherence. The fact that the lover saturates her sight (echoing the eclipse of Jesus' face) makes her not care about heaven and its values. Furthermore (perhaps), his being lost (damned) would make her glad to give up her salvation in order to share his fate, and were he saved, any possible separation would be, for her, the same thing as hell. The last stanza does not connect logically to what precedes it. The poem seems to return to the world of the living, and it seems to be saying that the lovers' complicated prospects and perhaps their shocking unconventionality make the future so uncertain that they can depend on only the small sustenance of their present narrow communication and tortured hopes. The short lines and abruptly rocking movement of the poem echo their struggles.

"My Life had stood – a Loaded Gun" (754) is an even more difficult poem, ending with what is probably the most difficult stanza in any of Dickinson's major poems. Defiantly joyous in tone – at least on the surface – until its almost tragic final stanza, this poem presents an allegory about the pursuit of personal identity and fulfillment through love, and yet it is quite possible that the joy of the poem conceals a satire directed back against the speaker, a satire which may be the chief clue to the meaning of the last stanza. The life of the person as a loaded gun probably stands for all of her potential as a person, perhaps creatively as well as sexually. Her being claimed by the owner suggests subservience to a lover as the only way to achieve selfhood – a stereotype of woman's position in society. Her powers are released by the owner-lover, and the landscape of the world rewards her by acknowledging her expression of his power. The Vesuvian face suggests the speaker's sexual release being read into the landscape, and perhaps also the joy on the face of the lover, who remains curiously uncharacterized throughout the poem. The nighttime scene in which the speaker-as-gun takes more pleasure in protecting the owner than in sleeping with him (the grammar makes it possible to conclude that she has not slept with him, or to conclude that she enjoys protecting him more than sharing his bed) gives to the sexual element a strange ambiguity, because she seems equally joyous at resuming her daytime role of releasing destruction. Just what she kills is difficult to say, but the yellow eye and emphatic thumb are sinister enough to suggest that the speaker is aware of something demeaning in her dependent, destructive, and self-denigrating role. The poem's joy, or pretended joy, dissolves in the last stanza. The speaker thinks that she may outlive the owner-lover, but she knows that in some sense she cannot. These lines appear to contradict one another completely. The qualification that the speaker-gun has "but the power to kill" undercuts the earlier celebration of her power.

Evidently her celebrating that power as something good is a delusion. The power to kill, then, does not give identity, and its satisfactions are misleading. The last line presents an absolute paradox. The speaker-gun's inability to die will make the owner-lover outlive her. The paradox can be resolved by assuming that *die* may have a special meaning. Quite possibly to die means to realize some kind of consummation or identity, including the sexual – to achieve the self by a discharge of energy more real than the act of totally serving another. If this is the case, the speaker-gun has never really lived and so the owner-lover must outlive her. Of course the specific fantasies that lie behind the poem are unrecoverable. The poem has been interpreted as a comment on the speaker's relationship with God or on her activity as a poet. Individual beliefs about psychological and sexual motives and symbols can influence the interpretation of this poem. Our interpretation of "In Winter in my Room" and "I started Early – took my Dog" may reinforce our view of this poem.

Although "There came a Day at Summer's full" (322) contains some painful elements, the kinds of fantasies that we have just examined receive a much more gentle, exuberant, and joyful treatment in it. The resignation seen in "I cannot live with You" here turns into a prelude to a triumph beyond death for a love that could not succeed on earth. This poem presents a more visual scene than both "I cannot live with You" and "My Life had stood – a Loaded Gun," but it is still clearly an allegorical scene, and there is no reason to assume that Emily Dickinson ever had an experience like the one it presents. The action occurs on the day of the summer solstice, usually June 21st, the longest day of the year, when the promise of spring, symbolically, if not literally, becomes the fullness of summer. The first two stanzas stress the spiritual triumph of this day for the speaker, which overshadows the fullness of nature and places her and her lover in a world entirely apart from it. She seems to be expressing surprise that nature carries on in its usual way without paying any attention to her great experience. Love is so intrinsic to their companionship that speaking of their love would be a kind of profanation, just as the idea that priestly garbs are essential to sacraments is a profanation. (Nature is brushed aside, and love substitutes both for it and for religion.) The lovers, excluding the world, become their own church and hold their own communion, an act which will prepare them for heaven. However, they are destined to part, but their parting will intensify their relationship. Still maintaining silence, they exchange crucifixes, which seem to substitute for wedding rings, perhaps guaranteeing union through suffering. Their betrothal – depending on how we interpret the grammar of the last stanza – will overcome the grave and give them a marriage in heaven. Probably these lines are saying that their suffering is the sufficient troth that will ensure their marriage. The last line can be read as modifying "marriage," or as describing their general troth and suffering. In this poem, the element of conflict and suffering is held in balance with, or made subservient to, the triumphs of love. The lovers' rapt attention to each other and their disregard of the world contribute to the poem's tone of affirmation. The conflicts dramatized in this poem lack the ambiguity of "I started Early – Took my Dog" and "My Life had stood – a Loaded Gun," where the sexual elements probably puzzled even the author-speaker. Dickinson seems to confront her longings more straightforwardly when she sees them as simple matters of separation.

In "If you were coming in the Fall" (511), Dickinson treats love-separation and hope for earthly or heavenly reunion in an even more straightforward manner. The poem's domestic images show Dickinson using the everyday and trivial to describe strong emotions, but these images also serve to suggest that the speaker is used to her situation. It is a part of her daily life, and she is able to take a detached, but not quite flippant, attitude towards it. The stress on geography implies a physical separation – she never sees the beloved. The image of a fly and the image of time as balls of yarn – these show that she is occupied by routine tasks while she is thinking about the beloved. In the third and fourth stanzas, she grows extravagant, imagining how easy it would be to wait out centuries, or to pass through death, if either would bring her the lover. The counting by hand and the tossed rind (which represents the act of dying) continue the domestic images, not only unifying the poem but reducing the vastness of time and death to something controllable. The last stanza says that since she has no idea how long she must wait for him, she is goaded like a person around whom a bee hovers. The goblin nature of the bee lends mystery and ambivalence to whatever she must suffer to be with her lover. The poem employs four parallel stanzas before its concluding fifth stanza, but rather than creating monotony these build up a pleasant suspense that is given a concentrated expression in the end, where one also senses a concentration of restiveness. This effective conclusion is quite different from the endings of the poems just discussed, and it helps to demonstrate that Dickinson uses a variety of tones and methods in her treatment of similar material.

We move now to a number of love poems in which the reality of consummation, in addition to the choice of a beloved, is more explicit and emphatic, but we should remember that disappointment, renunciation, and irony against the self may always lurk beneath the surface. "Mine – by the Right of the White Election!" (528), which is very popular with readers and anthologists, almost seems a concentration of the conclusions of her love poems. Gaining extraordinary emphasis from its lack of a main verb (which would logically appear in an implied statement such as "He is . . ."), its insistent parallelism, and its concentrated metaphors, this poem declares that a beloved person is the speaker's possession, although he is now physically absent and will be closer – if that is possible – only after death. "White Election" may refer to Emily Dickinson's typically white garb and to her sexual innocence. The prison is her isolation that cannot hide her dedication. "Vision" and "Veto," which critics sometimes use as caption descriptions of Dickinson's view of love, or even of her poetry as a whole, suggest the presence of love in the spirit intensified by the forbidding of its physical presence. Only the "grave's repeal" will give permanent confirmation to what she already somehow possesses. Although this poem has considerable appeal because of its exuberance and technical virtuosity, its somewhat hysterical tone may lessen its effectiveness. The poet's frenetic attitude may influence even our perception of the poem's central purpose, which is to celebrate the possession of a beloved person, by leading us to suspect that considerable doubt may lie behind its overly emphatic affirmation. The poem can also be interpreted as an affirmation of the speaker's assurance of God's choice of her for salvation ("white election"). We prefer our interpretation largely because the phrase "Vision and . . . Veto" echoes Dickinson's sense of an enforced separation from a beloved person.

Possession of an infinitely worshipped person is presented in a different manner in "Of all the Souls that stand create" (664). The subterfuge of life which we put behind at death may refer to the physical elusiveness of the beloved person, to the artificiality of social life, or to both. The notion of separating the before and the after, and the description of life as a process of shifting sands, suggest the greater reality and stability of the afterlife. The concentrated last four lines show an overlapping of the physical and the spiritual. Life is presented as being mistlike in that it obscures real values. One beloved person, a mere atom in all creation, will stand out from every other human being, but will be visible only as a spirit. The speaker rejoices in her preference as if it were an indication of her own superiority. Unlike many of her religiously oriented love poems, this one does no violence to Christian doctrine in its view of life, death, and love. This conventional set of mind contributes to the poem's detachment, for although other of her love poems insist that reunion will occur only in heaven, they still reflect a strong sense of concrete physical presence. Because this poem is so detached, as a result of its being intellectually demonstrative rather than personally dramatic, some readers may find the beloved figure somewhat vague and fatherly.

That Dickinson's hopes for becoming close to a lover fluctuated dramatically at times can be demonstrated by moving from "Of all the Souls that stand create" to two such different poems as "Wild Nights – Wild Nights!" (249) and "The Soul selects her own Society" (303), both among her best and most popular poems. In "Wild Nights – Wild Nights!" Dickinson expresses passionate longing for a loving physical intimacy with the specific person she is addressing. The scene is presented metaphorically and its water images remind us of details in "I started Early – Took my Dog" and "There came a Day at Summer's full." In "Wild Nights – Wild Nights!" she desires a fulfillment that in those poems is feared or looked forward to only after death. Here, the first stanza anticipates nights to be spent with a beloved. Both wildness and luxury are part of a shared, overflowing passion. In the second stanza, these nights become a reality, and the concentrated imagery shows that the wildness stands both for passion and for the threat to it from the socially forbidding world. She imagines herself, at the same time, at sea with love and in a protective harbor, and no longer does she need to traverse the sea of separation and prohibition. Sea and port paradoxically seem to merge. In the final stanza, this merging is suggested by "rowing in Eden," where the combination of sea and port corresponds to the physical reality of harbors, except for their exclusion of storms, and where "Eden" implies the attainment of paradise in this world, rather than after death. At this point, the sea as a place for mooring represents the beloved. The last line acknowledges again that Dickinson is describing a fantasy, not a reality, but in it there is a sigh of relief – assisted by the rhyme that echoes back to the first stanza – rather than a cry of desperation. The speaker as a mooring ship suggests a woman nestling against the body of a man and into his life. It is also a fitting symbol for the end of a quest. The suggestions of masculinity in this poem's speaker may reveal in Dickinson an urge to be active in creating a situation that she usually anticipates more passively.

The rarely anthologized but magnificent poem, "I had not minded – Walls" (398), which was added as an appendix to *Final Harvest* after its first edition, makes yet another interesting contrast to "Wild Nights – Wild Nights!" In this poem the emphasis is on the inaccessibility of a beloved person held at an impossible distance by the laws of society, which laws make a barrier that the speaker says she would find easy to penetrate if it were merely physical and as large as the universe. Perhaps in Dickinson's mind this was the same distance that her imagination joyously traversed in "Wild Nights – Wild Nights!"

"The Soul selects her own Society" (303) is a difficult poem that has been variously interpreted. It seems to stand midway between the yearning of "There came a Day at Summer's full," where fulfillment is hoped for in heaven, and the scene of almost-fulfilled desires in "Wild Nights." Here, Dickinson appears to assert that in some special and mysterious way she is always in the company of one person whom her soul has chosen as its only needed companion. The poem is written not in the usual first person of her love poems, but in a detached and meditative third person, until the last stanza where the speaker appears and comments on the third person figure of the first two stanzas. The "Soul" of the first line may at first appear to represent any person, but close examination shows that it is Dickinson herself, or the speaker of the poem, seen from a distance. Also "Society" at first may appear to be a large group of people, but in reality it is one person. "Divine Majority" paradoxically implies that one person or better yet – two people – have become more important than anyone else. The third line is probably a declaration that no others are present, but since Dickinson proposed the word "obtrude" as an alternative to "present," the line may be an imperative telling other people to stay away. In the second stanza, the soul, or essential self, sees people arriving in chariots, an elevated way of describing carriages (perhaps hinting at heavenly as well as at kingly status), but she indicates that she would not be moved even if an emperor asked for her attention. These figures may stand for people in general or for prospective suitors. In the last stanza, the switch to first person shows Dickinson quietly reveling in the strength of her renunciation. The ample nation is everyone available to her. The chosen one is the beloved whose spirit she lives with or has perhaps taken into herself by the power of imagination. "Valves of her attention" gives the soul the power of concentration. The soul has almost denied everything else in life to lock itself into its strange relationship with the chosen "one." "Stone" represents its complete rejection of the rest of the world. The alternating short-long lengths of the poem's lines, culminating in the two-syllable lines of the last stanza, parallels this closing down of attention and strengthens our sense of a painful but glorious triumph in the concluding lines. Unusually rich in sound effects, including alliteration, rhyme, and modulation of vowels, this is one of Dickinson's greatest successes in poetic technique. Some critics believe that the subject of this poem is the union of the soul with the muse or with God, rather than with a lover.

The idea of a spiritual union with a beloved person is more explicit in several other Dickinson poems, but none is as brilliant as "The Soul selects." Because in several of these poems Dickinson, or her speaker, refers to herself as wife or bride, these poems are sometimes called "the marriage group." However, they are not necessarily any more joyous than "The Soul selects." Probably "I'm 'wife'—I've finished that" (199) is the most revealing of these "marriage" poems. (We did not include "There came a Day" and "Mine—by the Right" here because they are about an anticipated rather than a fulfilled union.) This slow-paced poem has an eerie and detached tone. The placing of quotation marks around "wife" and "woman" suggests that these are chiefly social concepts related to status, or it may indicate that the speaker is changing the meaning of those concepts to suit herself. She regards her earlier pre-marriage state with scorn, implying that she has found her own safety without having gone through a conventional marriage. The soft eclipse of her imagined or spiritual marriage blurs the harsh light of what preceded it, although "eclipse" may also refer to the loss of individuality. The use of "folks" in her contrast between heaven and earth implies that her accomplishment has been easy to will or that it resembles the wish-fulfillment of a dream. Having exchanged pain for comfort, she seems astonished that it could be willed so easily. The paired question and assertion of the last two lines suggests a certain numbness reinforcing the implication that the whole process has been painful and reinforcing the poem's aura of unreality. The poet's attitude toward her triumph is ambiguous; she seems uncertain about its nature, and yet she is reluctant to explore her state further, as if through further questioning she might lose everything.

We find an even more intense mixture of feelings in another "marriage" poem, "Title divine – is mine!" (1072), one of Dickinson's most complex and ambiguous poems. Like other poems that we assign to the category of love, this one has also been interpreted as being about God, or poetry, or the achievement of selfhood. In our view, this poem, like "The Soul selects" and "I'm 'wife' – I've finished that," deals primarily with the fantasy of a spiritual marriage to a man from whom the speaker is physically separated. This time, however, she seems quite aware that the suffering is greater than the rewards, and that, in fact, the whole thing is a bitter delusion. The title of wife is divine for two reasons – because society considers it to be, and because it brings elevation. Possibly "divine" also indicates that this marriage exists only spiritually. The missing sign refers to the physical and social reality of marriage. "Acute degree" and "Empress of Calvary" are both paradoxical. The acuteness is the sharp angle of pain. "Calvary" is an elevating suffering, but still the worst suffering imaginable. She has gone through this marriage without the fearfully ecstatic loss of self that other women experience, but her loss is more terrible. In one day she has been born through love, has been made bride, and therefore been bridled like a horse, and has been shrouded, in the sense that her peculiar marriage is a kind of living death. Such a victory is triply ironic. She tries to pronounce the words of love and elevation proper to a real wife, but asks if her way – probably referring to her whole bitter poem – has caught the right tone. On the biographical level, perhaps this poem shows Dickinson's combination of doubts and affirmations about real marriage as much as it shows her anguish over her own ambivalent idea of a spiritual marriage.

Two lesser marriage poems, "She rose to His Requirement" (732) and "A Wife – at Daybreak I shall be" (461) are harder to interpret within the pattern of Dickinson's love poems. "She rose to His Requirement" (732) appears to describe an actual marriage in which a woman gives up the casual play of girlhood for the honorable status of wife. This new state, however, seems to be a considerable disappointment. The woman perhaps has not found the riches of fulfillment that she had expected. However, she allows herself no mention of her disappointments. The comparison of what she does not mention to both pearl and weed suggests that in the depths of the woman's soul there are both secret rewards and secret sufferings. Knowledge of these depths is assigned to the sea rather than to the woman, but the sea seems to be a symbol for part of the woman. This symbolic splitting of woman and sea implies that the woman has detached herself from her husband, and reaps, or faces, special rewards and punishments by herself. Very probably an attempt to look objectively at the rewards and losses of those real-life marriages in which Dickinson did not share, this poem may also contain parallels to her own condition as imagined wife and as poet.

"A Wife—at Daybreak I shall be" (461) places an anxious and almost desperate emphasis on that split between girlhood and the married state that has been a subject of other poems that we have discussed. The chronology here is somewhat overlapping, suggesting an anxious thrust towards a fulfilling future. The speaker alternates between expecting to move from girlhood to marriage and asserting that she has done so. In the second stanza, she repeats the pattern, this time rushing up the stairs of childhood towards her marriage. Now, however, the marriage seems to be in eternity or heaven. The poem may represent a suicidal impulse, or a blending of the idea of spiritual marriage with the idea of a union in heaven. In any case, the poem's repetitive method does not create the complexity of feeling of Dickinson's better and more dramatic poems about an imagined or future marriage.

The infrequently anthologized "I'm ceded—I've stopped being Theirs" (508) makes an interesting connection between the marriage poems and the poems about growth and personal identity. Here, there is no mention of marriage, but the speaker's progression from shallow girlhood, where she gained identity from her family and their values, to her fully realized potentiality in which she hears her true and self-given name, reveals striking parallels to the marriage poems. Her whole existence becomes full, and she is crowned. She has moved from a low rank to the highest imaginable rank. The implied doubts of "I'm 'wife,' I've finished that," the isolation of "The Soul selects," and the irony of "Title divine" are entirely absent from this poem. Probably the condition of a crowned queen here represents that being a poet gives her the feeling that she is a whole person. Thus we see illustrated one of the many thematic overlappings between her love poems and her poems on other subjects.

We have grouped Emily Dickinson's poems on social themes with her love poems partly because both types of her poetry stress her evaluation of people whom she observed. For many poets, society provides a context for their treatment of love, or perhaps a clear delineation of a world from which they withdraw into love. Dickinson's social satire criticizes all kinds of shallowness from which she fled to thoughts of love. Although early critics of Dickinson emphasized her neglect of the social scene, later critics have scrutinized her work to find every conceivable treatment of social themes. We confine ourselves here to mostly a few widely anthologized poems relating to society.

The very popular "I'm Nobody! Who are you!" (288), on the surface, may seem a slight performance, but it is not a superficial poem. On the biographical level, the poem perhaps reflects Dickinson's resentment of shallow writers who gain undeserved attention. Or she may be satirizing the character and situation of people who loom large in the eyes of society—people whom we call "somebodys." Taking assurance from the company of a fellow nobody, the speaker pretends to be worried that they will be held up to public shame for their failure to compete for attention. However, the sudden transition to a denunciation of "somebodys" suggests that if one gains notice as a nobody, it makes one into a kind of somebody. Clearly she prefers a position of invisibility, where she can take her own measure. The somebodys sit in the middle of bogs, a nasty representation of society, and the somebodys bellow to people who will admire them for their names alone. The poet seems to be mildly congratulating herself that unlike the vulgar and pretentious somebodys, she is shy and sensitive. The poem is jocular, amusing, and surely a bit defensive, and its psychology and satire are keen.

Turning her attention more critically to a more specific human type in "What Soft—Cherubic Creatures" (401), Dickinson produces one of her most popular and admired poems, although its unusual compression and its concentrated biblical allusions create difficulties for many readers. The poem is a portrait of excessively genteel women whose claims to status are based entirely on the externals of behavior, dress, and manners. Irony pervades the poem. The softness and cherubic nature of the ladies represents their pretended gentleness and false sweetness (with perhaps a hint at obesity). But the third and fourth lines show us that these women are detached from the real world around them and perhaps they even revel in this detachment. "Plush" describes the softness of upholstery material. The word is an adjective here converted into a noun for a cloth substance too soft to provoke anyone to assault it. Dimity is a dainty white cotton cloth and "dimity convictions" transfers the frailness and pretended innocence of the women's clothing to the women's beliefs. Perhaps we are to see them displaying their false values at religious services or in condescending acts of charity. Their convictions seem limited to a refined horror of ordinary human nature, perhaps in themselves as well as in others. The poem extends this shame about human nature to a shame about Christ, who was quite willing to put on human flesh. The antecedent of "It's" is human nature. The fisherman's degree, we think, refers not, as some critics suggest, to Peter, Christ's disciple, who was a fisherman, but to Christ himself, who, when He associated with fishermen, was a fisher of men. The last two lines state that the women's attitudes would make redemption (the Redeemer) ashamed of them and presumably deny them salvation. The switch from "soft" to "brittle" in reference to the women, that has troubled some critics, is easily explained as a shift from social demeanor to frail values, but also both of these adjectives suggest values that will not endure.

In "She dealt her pretty words like Blades" (479), Dickinson turns her attention to a single lady – perhaps one whom we can imagine imitating the softness of cherubic creatures until the lady has sufficient privacy to reveal a vindictive cutting edge. (Or it may be that she is a different but equally shallow human type.) The aggression here seems the reverse of the repression in some gentlewomen. Probably Dickinson wrote this poem with her sister-in-law, Susan, in mind. The pretty and glittering words suggest the pleasure which a clever woman takes in her speech while being at least partly aware of how much her words hurt those whom she is addressing. The poem's claim that the woman does not believe that she hurts must

64

describe a rationalization in the woman. Since the woman proudly sees herself as being like steel, she judges what she says to people as being properly corrective. Despite her implied denial, she realizes quite well the hurt she gives, but she adds to her original attack by scorning her victims for not exhibiting pain gracefully. The poem is very cleverly built. The first stanza is spoken in detached anger by an observer or a victim. The second stanza imitates the viewpoint of the vicious woman. The third stanza passes a cool judgment on the whole affair, first defending the victim's sensitivity and painful response, and then describing those defenses which finally lead hurt people to withdraw into a protective death-like state. The tone of the last two lines is somewhat jocular. In them, the speaker, drawing upon her own experience, claims a knowledge of suffering so keen that it is like death – a suffering which the attacker refuses to see.

The very popular "Much Madness is divinest Sense" (435) expresses just such a strong feeling of personal suffering, and it leaves the picture and nature of the cruel behavior which it attacks so generalized that one may not immediately notice its social satire. If we wish to make a biographical interpretation, we can note the relationship of its ideas of divinity and a majority to those of "The Soul selects her own Society," where a divine majority of two requires the shutting out of the ordinary majority. In this poem, the discerning eye represents the person who sees that going her own way and choosing her own values may lead to the intensest life, whereas choosing what the world calls sense may produce emptiness, or waste, or pretension, all of which are madness to a sensitive person. The fourth and fifth lines protest against the majority's dictating standards for personal values and conduct, as well as for the rest of society's organization. As she moves from personal situation to social dictatorship, the poet expresses an increasingly mocking anger. The last three lines imply the instruments, social ostracism or even the asylum or prison, which the majority uses to hold people in line. The last line confirms our earlier sense that the concealed speaker feels imprisoned. The poem is brilliantly constructed, with the first three lines illustrating the daring of independent souls, the last three lines showing how they are restricted, and the middle two lines providing the transition from the personal to the social level. This poem ritualizes the internalization of social bondage.

There are three interesting and brief glances at social situations in the poems, "The Popular Heart is a Cannon first" (1226), "The

65

Show is not the Show" (1206), and "This quiet Dust was Gentlemen and Ladies" (813). "The Popular Heart is a Cannon first" seems to describe the celebration of a national holiday, possibly the Fourth of July, when patriotic types fire off cannons, march with drums, and get drunk. It may, however, be chiefly about the drilling of militia soldiers. The second stanza satirizes their sinking into a drunken stupor, and their lying in ditches and jail and ridicules their activities as an improper memorial for historical events.

"The Show is not the Show" (1206) presents more objectively the kind of social criticism shown in "I'm Nobody! Who are You?" Attendance at a public entertainment brings out the showiness or pretense of those who attend more than it reveals anything spectacular in the event. In lines three and four, she seems to be saying that her neighbors are like zoo creatures to her, and the last two lines imply that her view of them is fair because her neighbors are probably making a similar judgment of her.

"This quiet Dust was Gentlemen and Ladies" (813) was a popular Dickinson poem several decades ago, when in the public eye her superficial wit sometimes eclipsed her deeper insights. It makes, perhaps, a gentle companion piece for "What Soft – Cherubic Creatures." Here, the poem looks back at both young and old who were socially pretentious and given to shallow pursuits. Instead of the shocking contrast of dead people and continuing nature that we find in many Dickinson poems on death, this one attributes a certain superficiality or pointlessness to the cycle of nature. The poem itself expresses comic relief, perhaps as if the speaker were glad not to be troubled about either social pursuits or death. It is also possible that the poet in a neutral or slightly elegaic tone is saying not much more than that the cycle of nature resembles the cycle of man.

What may be Dickinson's most popular poem on a social theme, "I like to see it lap the Miles" (585), is devoid of both people and an explicit social scene. However, its satirical treatment of the invasion of her quarter of the world by a mechanical monster that seems to have delighted everyone else but her can be seen as a satire on the advance of industrial society. The poem domesticates a railroad train by presenting it as a horse. The idea of speed is satirized by making the train into a licking animal, while the impersonality of the train's fueling is converted into feeding. In the second and third stanzas, the train-as-horse takes on somewhat disagreeable human qualities as it enjoys its conquest of the landscape while making a racket that the speaker finds horrid. In the last stanza it reaches its goal, and the conjunction of "docile and omnipotent" shows it as both under man's control and potentially breaking loose—or perhaps lending its omnipotence to the humans who have created it. The speaker seems to sigh with relief at the end, perhaps reflecting Dickinson's difficulty in dealing with social subjects.

Quite possibly, Dickinson could not apply her talents to social subjects with much force because they did not arouse in her the kinds of emotion which she struggles to express and control in her best love poems. However, such triumphs of satire as "What Soft—Cherubic Creatures" and "She dealt her pretty words like Blades" are partly inspired by angers that resemble the tensions in her love poems.

Suffering and Growth

Emily Dickinson's poems often express joy about art, imagination, nature, and human relationships, but her poetic world is also permeated with suffering and the struggle to evade, face, overcome, and wrest meaning from it. Many of her poems about poetry, love, and nature that we have discussed also treat suffering. Suffering is involved in the creative process, it is central to unfulfilled love, and it is part of her ambivalent response to the mysteries of time and nature. Suffering also plays a major role in her poems about death and immortality, just as death often appears in poems that concentrate on suffering. Her poems on this subject can be divided into three groups: those focusing on deprivation as a cause of suffering, those in which anguish leads to disintegration, and those in which suffering—or painful struggles—bring compensatory rewards or spiritual growth.

When Emily Dickinson's poems focus on the fact of and progress of suffering, she rarely describes its causes. Looking back at the love poem "I cannot live with You" (640) and the socially satirical "She dealt her pretty words like Blades" (479), we find passages about specific suffering, but this is not their central subject. However, the evidence that she experienced love-deprivation suggests that it lies behind many of her poems about suffering—poems such as "Renunciation—is a piercing Virtue" (745) and "I dreaded that first Robin so"

(348). In "Renunciation—is a piercing Virtue" (745), Emily Dickinson seems to be writing about abandoning the hope of possessing a beloved person. However, she is more abstract here than in her poems where a lover is visible, and she is not clear about the final meaning of her painful experience. The first four lines present renunciation as both elevating and agonizing. The alternating line length gives the poem a slow, hesitating movement, like the struggles of a mind in torment. The speaker hopes that her renunciation will be rewarded and the use of "Not now" for "but not now" emphasizes her effort. The eyes that are sunrise resemble the face that would put out Jesus' eyes in "I cannot live with You," but this passage is more painful, for the force of "piercing" carries over to the description of eyes being put out and suggests a blinding not so much of the beloved person as of the speaker. She is drawing back, she claims, from the sacrilege of valuing something more than she values God, a person who is like the sunrise. In the last seven lines, the speaker is struggling to develop and express her ideas. She chooses something which she does not want in order to justify herself—not to others (such as God) but to *herself*, and this striving for justification is done less for the present moment than for some future time. "Larger function" means a clearer scheme or idea about existence—one which explains the meaning of mortality—in which her present, selfish desires will appear small. When she is dead, she will finally understand the limitations of her present vision. At the conclusion of the poem, she is still staggering in pain, and the whole poem shows that she has only partial faith in the piercing virtue of renunciation. Her all-encompassing suffering remains a mystery.

The image of piercing which we have just examined resembles Emily Dickinson's typical image of Calvary, which appears in "I dreaded that first Robin so" (348), where the speaker's description of herself as Queen of Calvary suggests a suffering stemming from forbidden love. But this can only be speculation, and Emily Dickinson seems to take pleasure in making a lengthy parade of unspecified sufferings. Her dread of the first robin shows that her bereavement occurred before spring came, or that it was endurable during winter. Now she fears that the contrast of spring's beauty and vitality with her sorrow will intensify her pain. The poem refers repeatedly to her earlier anticipations. She feared that the bird's song and the blooming flowers would torture her by contrast to her situation. Her thoughts of the grass and bees are a bit different, however, for she says that she would want to hide in the grass, and though she implies that the bees liveliness would be a threat, her reference to their "dim countries" is envious. Her having rehearsed her anticipations helped her face spring's arrival. The last two stanzas are somewhat lighter in tone. The failures of creatures and flowers to stay away gives her some pleasure, for she now makes of them her own mournful parade. The image of Queen of Calvary is a deliberate self-dramatization. The creatures and flowers, she insists, are indifferent to her pain, but she is able to project enough sympathy into them to make the experience almost rewarding. She seems aware of the posing dramatized in her lifting childish plumes. The poem expresses anger against nature's indifference to her suffering, but it may also implicitly criticize her self-pity.

Among Emily Dickinson's less popular poems are several about childhood deprivation. Here she is explicit about the sources of suffering, but the poems are less forceful than her general treatments of suffering, and their anger against the people they criticize is weaker than the anger in "What Soft – Cherubic Creatures" and "She dealt her pretty words like Blades." In "It would have starved a Gnat" (612), Emily Dickinson seems to be charging that when she was a child her family denied her spiritual nourishment and recognition. The pervasive metaphor of a starving insect, plus repetition and parallelism, gives special force to the poem. Something as tiny as a gnat would have starved upon what she was fed as a child, food representing emotional sustenance. The phrase "live so small" converts the idea of spiritual nourishment into the idea of a self compelled to remain unobtrusive, undemanding, and unindividual. The image of hunger as a claw shows the natural strength of the child's needs, and the analogy to a leech and a dragon, using Emily Dickinson's typical yoking of the large and the small, dramatizes the painful tenacity of hunger. In the third stanza, she is explicit about the denial of individuality, and she adds a twist to the gnat comparison by showing that the tiny insect's freedom gives it a strength (and implied size) which is denied to her. The envy of the gnat's self-destructiveness, as it beats out its trapped life against the windowpane, suggests a suicidal urge in the speaker, and the poem ends on an unfortunate note of self-pity.

In "I had been hungry, all the Years" (579), Emily Dickinson shows one possible result of the kind of upbringing which she described (probably an autobiographical exaggeration) in "It would have starved a Gnat." Here, the symbolic meaning of food remains indeterminate. The first two stanzas contrast food seen through windows which the speaker passed with the spare sustenance which she could expect at home. The third stanza implies that she has been dining less at home than with the birds, who probably represent the world of imagination and art as well as the world of nature. She finally finds herself inside another dwelling where she is offered an abundance of food and drink. This image probably represents a warmth of society denied to her at home. Her character, however, has been formed by deprivation, and her description of herself as ill and rustic, and therefore out of place amidst grandeur, shows her feelings of inferiority or insecurity. However, the pleasure she has taken in sharing crumbs with birds suggests that there is something distinctive and valuable in her character. In the last stanza she finds the world of social abundance to be artificial and not capable of delivering the kind of food which she needs, and so she rejects it. However, she is probably aware that it is an exaggeration to say that her hunger disappears when food becomes available. Several critics have said that the yearning here is for affection and sexual experience, but no matter what the underlying desires, Emily Dickinson is expressing a strange and touching preference for a withdrawn way of life; this is a variation on the fervent rejection of society in poems such as "I dwell in Possibility" and in a few of her love poems.

In the rarely anthologized "A loss of something ever felt I" (959), a deep sense of deprivation and alienation is expressed rather gently. In the first two stanzas, Emily Dickinson recalls a childhood feeling that she had lost something precious and undefinable, and that no one knew of her loss. She lived very much apart even as she associated with people. In the last two stanzas, she describes her situation with a tender and accepting sadness that implies a forgiveness for those who have hurt her. The "delinquent palaces" are the ideal conditions or loving relationships which she never found, but her calling them, rather than herself, "delinquent" suggests that they, and not she, are responsible for the failure. The speculation in the last stanza is a further clue to the psychology of her deprivation. If she is searching for the kingdom of heaven, she wants something that was never available to her in childhood or adulthood. This contradicts her implied accusations against others and indicates both that she forgives those who hurt her and recognizes that her expectations were impossibly high. In everyday terms, the mental formula would be: why should I blame you for not giving me what really isn't available on this earth? – a formula which can contain much repressed anger.

Among Emily Dickinson's poems in which anguish goes on indefinitely, or is transformed into protective numbness, are two fine epigrammatic poems. In treating this subject, Emily Dickinson rarely hints at the causes of suffering, apparently preferring to keep personal motives hidden, and she concentrates on the self-contained nature of the pain. However, close examination sometimes reveals possible causes of the suffering.

"Pain – has an Element of Blank" (650) deals with a self-contained and timeless suffering, mental rather than physical. The personification of pain makes it identical with the sufferer's life. The blank quality serves to blot out the origin of the pain and the complications that pain brings. The second stanza insists that such suffering is aware only of its continuation. Just as the sufferer's life has become pain, so time has become pain. Its present is an infinity which remains exactly like the past. This infinity, and the past which it reaches back to, are aware only of an indefinite future of suffering. The description of the suffering self as being enlightened is ironic, for although this enlightenment is the only light in the darkness, it is still characterized by suffering.

"The heart asks Pleasure – first" (536) appears to be simple, but close study reveals complexities. The first of its eight lines deals with the desire for pleasure, and the remaining seven lines treat pain and the desire for its relief. This proportion may at first suggest that pleasure is being sought as a relief from pain, but this idea is unlikely. The rapid shift from a desire for pleasure to a pursuit of relief combines with the slightly childlike voice of the poem to show that the hope for pleasure in life quickly yields to the universal fact of pain, after which a pursuit of relief becomes life's center. Such relief is pursued in four stages. To ask for an excuse from pain means either to dismiss it or to leave it behind, like a child asking to be excused from a duty. Anodynes (medicines that relieve pain) are a metaphor for activities that lessen suffering. The hesitant slowness of the phrase "deaden suffering" conveys the cramped nature of such ease. The cumulative "and then" phrases imitate a child's recital of a series of desired things. The child has doubts about the procedure being described and the adult speaker knows that it will fail. The hope that sleep will relieve pain resembles advice given to unhappy children. The Inquisitor stands for God, who creates a world of suffering but won't allow us to die until He is ready. He is being compared to the torturers of the medieval Inquisition, although it is also possible that the Inquisitor represents a sense of guilt on the part of the speaker.

"The heart asks Pleasure – first" takes a passive stance towards suffering, but it also criticizes a world that makes people suffer. Such attitudes are shown more subtly in "After great pain, a formal feeling comes" (341), Emily Dickinson's most popular poem about suffering, and one of her greatest poems. As are the two poems just discussed, it is told in the third person, but it seems very personal. The speaker watches her suffering protagonist from a distance and uses symbols to intensify the psychic splitting through the images of the nerves, heart, and feet. The pain must be psychological, for there is no real damage to the body and no pursuit of healing. The "formal feeling" suggests the protagonist's withdrawal from the world, a withdrawal which implies a criticism of those who have made her suffer. A funeral goes on inside her, with the nerves acting both as mourners and as a tombstone. Reference to the stiff heart, whose sense of time has been destroyed, continues the feeling of arrest. Since Emily Dickinson capitalizes words almost arbitrarily, one cannot know for certain if "He" refers to Christ. The grammatical reference is more continuous if "He" refers to the heart itself, although it may refer to both Christ *and* the heart. The heart feels so dead and alienated from itself that it asks if it is really the one that suffered, and also if the crushing blow came recently or centuries earlier. Time feels dissolved – as if the sufferer has always been just as she is now.

In the second stanza, the protagonist is sufficiently alive and desirous of relief to walk around. She walks in a circle as an expression of frustration and because she has nowhere to go, but her feet are unfeeling. Her path, and her feet as well, are like wood – that is, they are insensitive to what is beneath and around them. Almost from its beginning, the poem has been dramatizing a state of emotional shock that serves as a protection against pain. As the second stanza ends, this stance becomes explicit, the feet and the walking now standing for the whole suffering self which grows contented with its hardened condition. "Quartz contentment" is one of Emily Dickinson's most brilliant metaphors, combining heaviness, density, and earthiness with the idea of contentment, which is usually thought to be mellow and soft. "The hour of lead" is another brilliant metaphor, in which time, scene, and body fuse into something heavy, dull, immovable. As does "quartz contentment," this figure of speech implies that such protection requires a terrible sacrifice. The last eight lines suggest that such suffering may prove fatal, but if it does not, it will be remembered in the same way in which people who are freezing to death remember the painful process leading to their final moment. In reality, however, they could not remember the moment of letting go which precedes death unless they were rescued soon after they slipped into unconsciousness. Perhaps Emily Dickinson is depicting the feeling that rescue, for her, is unlikely, or she may be voicing a call for rescue. But a sense of terrible alienation from the human world, analogous to the loneliness of people freezing to death, pervades the poem. The last line is particularly effective in its combining of shock, growing insensitivity, and final relief, which parallels the overall structure of the poem. The varied line lengths, the frequent heavy pauses within the lines, and the mixture of slant and full rhymes all contribute to the poem's formal slowness. This labored movement of the lines reinforces the thematic movement of the poem from pain to a final, dull resignation.

Although most critics think that "I felt a Funeral, in my Brain" (280) is about death, we see it as a dramatization of mental anguish leading to psychic disintegration and a final sinking into a protective numbness like that portrayed in "After great pain." But the poem is difficult to interpret. In "After great pain," the funeral elements are subordinate to a scene of mental suffering. In this poem, the whole psychological drama is described as if it were a funeral. This funeral is a symbol of an intense suffering that threatens to destroy the speaker's life but at last destroys only her present, unbearable consciousness. The poem offers no hints about the causes of her suffering, although her self-torment seems stronger than in "After great pain." The fourth line is especially difficult, for the phrase "breaking through," in regard to mental phenomena, usually refers to something becoming clear, an interpretation which does not fit the rest of the poem. If "sense" is taken as paralleling the "plank in reason" which later breaks, then "breaking through" can mean to collapse or shatter. The formal and treading mourners probably represent self-accusations strong enough to drive the speaker towards madness. But she is slow in getting there. The service continues, the coffin-like box symbolizing the death of the accused self that can no longer endure torment. Now the whole universe is like a church, with its heavens a bell. Unable to escape from her terrifying consciousness, she feels as if only she and the universe exist. All sounds pour into her silence. This is a condition close to madness, a loss of self that comes when one's relationship to people and nature feels broken, and individuality becomes a burden. At last, the desired numbness arrives. Reason, the ability to think and know, breaks down, and she plunges into an abyss. The worlds she strikes as she descends are her past experiences, both those she would want to hold onto and those that burden her with pain. Then she loses consciousness and is presumably at some kind of peace. The poem's regular rhythms work well with their insistent ritual, and the repeated trochaic words "treading – treading" and "beating – beating" oppose the iambic meter, adding a rocking quality.

Many images and motifs from "After great pain" and "I felt a Funeral" appear in varying guises in the less popular but brilliant "It was not Death, for I stood up" (510). The first two stanzas describe a terrible experience which is composed of neither death nor night, frost nor fire, but which we soon learn has qualities of them all. The bells are like those in "I felt a Funeral." The frost resembles the freezing in "After great pain," and the standing figures resemble the funereal ones in both those poems. Next, the speaker likens herself to corpses ready for burial, paralleling the deathlike images of those poems. In the third stanza, she describes a figure robbed of its individuality and forced to fit a frame – perhaps the standards of others. The mention of midnight contrasts the fullness of noon (a fullness of terror rather than of joy) to the midnight of social- and self-denial. In the fifth stanza, she compares her situation to a deserted and sterile landscape, where the earth's vitality is being cancelled. In the last stanza, she switches the simile and shows herself at sea – a desolated and freezing sea. Her condition here is worse than despair, for despair implies that hope and salvation were once available and now have been lost. She has no hope; her terrible feeling extends backwards as well as forward into emptiness. But although the self is oppressed and at the mercy of warring emotions and torments, the experience seems distanced. The ritualization of how the world persecutes her, the symbolizing of her suffering by landscape and seascape, and the analytical ordering of the material suggest some control over a suffering which she describes as irremediable.

"Twas like a Maelstrom, with a notch" (414) is an interesting variation on Emily Dickinson's treatment of destruction's threat. This poem employs neither the third person of "After great pain" nor the first person of "I felt a Funeral" and "It was not death"; instead, it is told in the second person, which seems to imply involvement in, and yet distance from, an experience that almost destroyed the speaker. The speaker appears threatened by psychic disintegration, although a few critics believe that the subject is the terror of death. For analysis, the poem can be divided into three parallel parts, plus a conclusion: the first two stanzas; the second two stanzas; the fifth stanza and the first two lines of the last stanza; and then the final two lines. In each of the three major sections, the speaker—who addresses herself with a generalizing "you"—is brought to the brink of destruction and then is suddenly spared. In the first section, her torturer is a murderous device designed to spill boiling water, or to pull her by the hem of her gown into a cauldron. The experience, however, turns out to be a nightmare from which she awakens. In the second section, the torturer is a goblin or a fiend who measures the time until it can seize her and tear her to pieces with its beastlike paws. She reacts stiffly and numbly—as in other poems—until God forces the satanic torturer to release her. God seems to act by whim—just barely remembering a task that ought to greatly concern him. In the third section, the torturer is a judicial process which leads her out to execution. The "luxury of doubt" in which she had been imprisoned is luxurious because it, at least, offers some hope of freedom from a miserable condition. But the prison from which she has been led cannot be the same thing as the forces that have been threatening to destroy her. Probably the prison is experienced as a realm of conflict, and the torturer-executioner who appears in three different guises is the possibility that her conflicts will drive her mad and kill her by making her completely self-alienated. In the last section, she is offered not freedom but a reprieve, implying that the whole process may start again. That is why she cannot tell if 1) being destroyed and leaving her suffering behind, or 2) going on with a life which faces constant threat, causes the greater anguish. This poem probably treats the same kind of alienation, lovelessness, and self-accusation found in "After great pain" and "I felt a Funeral."

"I read my sentence—steadily" (412) illustrates how difficult it can be to pin down Emily Dickinson's themes and tones. The poem fits the category of suffering for several reasons: it provides a bridge between Emily Dickinson's poems about suffering and those about the fear of death; it contains anxiety and threat resembling that of several poems just discussed; and its stoicism relates it to poems in which suffering is creative. Although the sentence delivered to the poem's speaker appears to be death, this interpretation creates difficulties. First, few of us have any clear idea of when we will die. Second, the poem's mockery of the judicial formula accompanying a death sentence is hard to connect to anything except a criminal's execution. Third, the soul's increasing familiarity with the inevitability of death and its tranquility do not go well with the anticipation of a definite time of death. The apparent pun on "matter" in the final line is troublesome, for if the word refers to the body as well as to the trial, the first meaning contradicts the indication that death is passing her by for the time being. These problems can be partly solved by seeing the drama as being dreamlike. In this view, the sentence to a specific time and manner of death may symbolize death's inevitability, and the temporal confusion at the end may represent the double-time of a dream, in which one lives on past an event and then continues to expect it to reoccur. The crime of the speaker would be merely having been born, and the mocking would be directed against an inexplicably cruel God. This interpretation is reasonable but makes it hard to account for the speaker's understated stoicism.

An alternate view is that the sentence is to a living-death—its date immediate, its manner her present suffering, and its shame the result of her feelings of unworthiness. Her scorn of the jury's piety suggests her anger at the notion that mercy could mitigate her suffering and shame. Knowing that all she has left is death, she comforts herself with the thought that its final stroke will not be novel. She and death need no public show of familiarity—she because of her pride and stoicism, and he because his power makes a display unnecessary and demeaning. They are equally cheerful and cold. This interpretation may not seem plausible on an initial reading of the poem; however, it accounts for more of the details than does a more conventional interpretation.

As we have seen, several of Emily Dickinson's poems about poetry and art reflect her belief that suffering is necessary for creativity. Poems on love and on nature suggest that suffering will lead to a fulfillment for love or that the fatality which man feels in nature elevates him and sharpens his sensibilities. Similar ideas appear in many poems about immortality. Emily Dickinson's ideas about the creative power of suffering resemble Ralph Waldo Emerson's doctrine of compensation, succinctly stated by him in a poem and an essay, each called "Compensation." According to this view, every apparent evil has a corresponding good, and good is never brought to birth without evil. A version of this idea appears in Emily Dickinson's four-line poem "A Death blow is a Life blow to Some" (816), whose concise paradox puzzles some readers. The "death blow" in this poem is not death literally. If the subject were salvation beyond death, the poem would have no drama. Emily Dickinson is writing about a select group of people whom she observes and who represent part of herself. She is struck by their transformation. The death blow is an assault of suffering, mental or physical, which forces them to rally all of their strength and vitality until they are changed. The first two lines present the basic observation. The second two lines look back at what would have gone on with a living death. Their suffering, therefore, becomes a matter of great good luck. Good and evil are held in balance.

Emily Dickinson takes a more limited view of suffering's benefits in "I like a look of Agony" (241). The speaker is an observer, but the anger of the poem suggests that she may see something of herself in the suffering of other people. She is a person who has been disgusted by artificiality and, therefore, she treasures the genuine. The first line is a deliberate challenge to conventionality. She is willing to praise what people hate in order to express her disgust with the sham that can go with everyday values. People who are truly convulsed are not acting. Several critics take the poem's subject to be death. We disagree – despite the obvious allusion to the crucifixion in the last two lines. The poem seems designed to show mounting anger. The second stanza rushes impetuously from the idea of terrible suffering to the absolute of death, as if the speaker were demanding that we face the worst consequences of suffering – death, in order to achieve authenticity.

Emily Dickinson's most famous poem about compensation, "Success is counted sweetest" (67), is more complicated and less cheerful.

It proceeds by inductive logic to show how painful situations create knowledge and experience not otherwise available. The poem opens with a generalization about people who never succeed. They treasure the idea of success more than do others. Next, the idea is given additional physical force by the declaration that only people in great thirst understand the nature of what they need. The use of "comprehend" about a physical substance creates a metaphor for spiritual satisfaction. Having briefly introduced people who are learning through deprivation, Emily Dickinson goes on to the longer description of a person dying on a battlefield. The word "host," referring to an armed troop, gives the scene an artificial elevation intensified by the royal color purple. These victorious, or seemingly victorious, people understand the nature of victory much less than does a person who has been denied it and lies dying. His ear is forbidden because it must strain to hear and will soon not hear at all. Pain lends clarity to the perception of victory. The bursting of strains near the moment of death emphasizes the greatness of sacrifice. This is a harsh poem. It asks for agreement with an almost cruel doctrine, although its harshness is often overlooked because of its crisp pictorial quality and its pretended cheerfulness. On the biographical level, it can be seen as a celebration of the virtues and rewards of Emily Dickinson's renunciatory way of life, and as an attack on those around her who achieved wordly success.

Emily Dickinson sometimes writes in a more genial and less harsh manner about suffering as a stimulus to growth. Two examples of this approach are the rarely anthologized "Revolution is the Pod" (1082) and "Growth of Man—like Growth of Nature" (750). Most of the few critical comments on "Revolution is the Pod" take its subject to be the revitalization of liberty. This is quite reasonable, although in the bulk of her poems and letters, Dickinson gives almost no attention to politics. However, the stress on individual in the first stanza suggests the possibility that Emily Dickinson is thinking about personal renewal as much as social renewal. Also, most of her nature metaphors that represent human activities are about individual growth. In any case, this exuberant poem begins by celebrating liberation and creation, both important values to a poet who chafed against restrictions and ordered her life through her writing. The second stanza continues the central metaphor of a seed-pod and a flower for society and self, and it offers the painful caution that they must undergo death and decay if, as the third stanza says, they are not to remain torpid. The function of revolution, then, like suffering, is to test and revive whatever may have become dead without our knowing it.

"Growth of Man – like Growth of Nature" (750) is a slower moving and more personal poem. It declares that personal growth is entirely dependent on inner forces. External circumstances may reveal its genuineness but they do not create it. The poem praises determination, personal faith, and courage in the face of opposition. The audience that looks on but can offer no help, described in the last stanza, is disembodied, even for Emily Dickinson's mental world. Surely it is a sign that she often felt that she could receive no help from the outside and must find her own way. Nevertheless, the poem seems to distort reality, although its quietness makes this quality unobtrusive.

Although the difficult "This Consciousness that is aware" (822) deals with death, it is at least equally concerned with discovery of personal identity through the suffering that accompanies dying. The poem opens by dramatizing the sense of mortality which people often feel when they contrast their individual time-bound lives to the world passing by them. Word order in the second stanza is inverted. The speaker anticipates moving between experience and death – that is, from experience into death by means of the experiment of dying. Dying is an experiment because it will test us, and allow us, and no one else, to know if our qualities are high enough to make us survive beyond death. The last stanza offers a summary that makes the death experience an analogy for other means of gaining self-knowledge in life. Neither boastful nor fearful, this poem accepts the necessity of painful testing.

"My Cocoon tightens – Colors tease" (1099) is both a lighter and a sadder treatment of the pursuit of growth. Several critics take its subject to be immortality. Its metaphor of the self as a butterfly, desiring both power and freedom, makes us think that it is about the struggle for personal growth. In the first stanza, the speaker is restricted but is faintly hopeful, and she contrasts her present limitations with her inner capacity. In the second stanza, she expresses a yearning for freedom and for the power to survey nature and feel at home with it. These personal qualities and this symbolic landscape represent life and its experiences as much, or more, than the achieving of paradise. In the last stanza, the speaker's hope for growth changes into a state of bafflement. She cannot read in herself, or nature, the formula which will allow her to make the right transformation, and she remains both puzzled and aspiring.

The rarely anthologized "Dare you see a Soul *at the White Heat?*" (365) is an unconstrained celebration of growth through suffering, though a few critics think that the poem is about love or the speaker's relationship to God. Addressed to the reader, the poem invites us to see a soul being transformed inside a furnace. When this soul is able to stand the suffering of fire, it will emerge white hot. The purified ore stands for transformed personal identity. At line nine, the poem divides into a second part. Here, the speaking voice is that of someone who has undergone such a transformation and can joyously affirm the availability of a change like its own for anyone willing to undergo it. The blacksmith's forge is described as a symbol, providing a metaphor within a metaphor. Just as small villages always have a blacksmith, so every soul has in it the possibility of passing through the fires of rebirth. The last four lines return to the poem's initial exuberance, and as the speaker sees the changed souls rising from their forges, she is thinking once more of her own triumph.

"The Brain – is wider than the Sky" (632) has puzzled and troubled many readers, probably because its surface statements fly so boldly in the face of accepted ideas about man's relationship to God. The three stanzas make parallel statements, but there is a significant variation in the third. The first stanza declares, with a deliberate defiance of ordinary perception, that the small human brain is larger than the wide sky, and that it can contain both the sky and all of the self. Emily Dickinson seems to be asserting that imagination or spirit can encompass, or perhaps give, the sky all of its meaning. The second stanza repeats the theme but lends it a fresh power through the metaphor of sponges absorbing buckets, which may suggest the poet's internalization of reality. The third stanza tries to outdo the earlier ones in overstatement. The "just" comparing the weight of the brain and of God is designed to show that the speaker is not boasting, but that she has taken a precise measure and can present her findings with offhand assurance. This stanza seems to claim for the human spirit equal status with the creative force in the universe, although possibly Emily Dickinson is merely suggesting that all human knowledge comes from God. Emily Dickinson's ideas here may resemble her most extravagant claims for the poet and the human imagination. We have placed the poem with those on growth because its exuberance conveys a sense of relief, accomplishment, and self-assertion.

Death, Immortality, and Religion

Even a modest selection of Emily Dickinson's poems reveals that death is her principal subject; in fact, because the topic is related to many of her other concerns, it is difficult to say how many of her poems concentrate on death. But over half of them, at least partly, and about a third centrally, feature it. Most of these poems also touch on the subject of religion, although she did write about religion without mentioning death. Other nineteenth-century poets, Keats and Whitman are good examples, were also death-haunted, but few as much as Emily Dickinson. Life in a small New England town in Dickinson's time contained a high mortality rate for young people; as a result, there were frequent death-scenes in homes, and this factor contributed to her preoccupation with death, as well as her withdrawal from the world, her anguish over her lack of romantic love, and her doubts about fulfillment beyond the grave. Years ago, Emily Dickinson's interest in death was often criticized as being morbid, but in our time readers tend to be impressed by her sensitive and imaginative handling of this painful subject.

Her poems centering on death and religion can be divided into four categories: those focusing on death as possible extinction, those dramatizing the question of whether the soul survives death, those asserting a firm faith in immortality, and those directly treating God's concern with people's lives and destinies.

The very popular "I heard a Fly buzz—when I died" (465) is often seen as representative of Emily Dickinson's style and attitudes. The first line is as arresting an opening as one could imagine. By describing the moment of her death, the speaker lets us know that she has already died. In the first stanza, the death-room's stillness contrasts with a fly's buzz that the dying person hears, and the tension pervading the scene is likened to the pauses within a storm. The second stanza focuses on the concerned onlookers, whose strained eyes and gathered breath emphasize their concentration in the face of a sacred event: the arrival of the "King," who is death. In the third stanza, attention shifts back to the speaker, who has been observing her own death with all the strength of her remaining senses. Her final willing of her keepsakes is a psychological event, not something she speaks. Already growing detached from her surroundings, she is no longer interested in material possessions; instead, she leaves behind whatever of herself people can treasure and remember. She is getting ready to guide herself towards death. But the buzzing fly intervenes at the last instant; the phrase "and then" indicates that this is a casual event, as if the ordinary course of life were in no way being interrupted by her death. The fly's "blue buzz" is one of the most famous pieces of synesthesia in Emily Dickinson's poems. This image represents the fusing of color and sound by the dying person's diminishing senses. The uncertainty of the fly's darting motions parallels her state of mind. Flying between the light and her, it seems to both signal the moment of death and represent the world that she is leaving. The last two lines show the speaker's confusion of her eyes and the windows of the room—a psychologically acute observation because the windows' failure is the failure of her own eyes that she does not want to admit. She is both distancing fear and revealing her detachment from life.

Critics have disagreed about the symbolic fly, some claiming that it symbolizes the precious world being left behind and others insisting that it stands for the decay and corruption associated with death. Although we favor the first of these, a compromise is possible. The fly may be loathsome, but it can also signify vitality. The synesthetic description of the fly helps depict the messy reality of dying, an event that one might hope to find more uplifting. The poem portrays a typical nineteenth-century death-scene, with the onlookers studying the dying countenance for signs of the soul's fate beyond death, but otherwise the poem seems to avoid the question of immortality.

In "This World is not Conclusion" (501), Emily Dickinson dramatizes a conflict between faith in immortality and severe doubt. Her earliest editors omitted the last eight lines of the poem, distorting its meaning and creating a flat conclusion. The complete poem can be divided into two parts: the first twelve lines and the final eight lines. It starts by emphatically affirming that there is a world beyond death which we cannot see but which we still can understand intuitively, as we do music. Lines four through eight introduce conflict.

Immortality is attractive but puzzling. Even wise people must pass through the riddle of death without knowing where they are going. The ungrammatical "don't" combined with the elevated diction of "philosophy" and "sagacity" suggests the petulance of a little girl. In the next four lines, the speaker struggles to assert faith. Puzzled scholars are less admirable than those who have stood up for their beliefs and suffered Christlike deaths. The speaker wants to be like them. Her faith now appears in the form of a bird who is searching for reasons to believe. But available evidence proves as irrelevant as twigs and as indefinite as the directions shown by a spinning weathervane. The desperation of a bird aimlessly looking for its way is analagous to the behavior of preachers whose gestures and hallelu-jahs cannot point the way to faith. These last two lines suggest that the narcotic which these preachers offer cannot still their *own* doubts, in addition to the doubts of others.

In "I know that He exists" (338), Emily Dickinson, like Herman Melville's Captain Ahab in *Moby-Dick*, shoots darts of anger against an absent or betraying God. This poem also has a major division and moves from affirmation to extreme doubt. However, its overall tone differs from that of "This World is not Conclusion." The latter poem shows a tension between childlike struggles for faith and the too easy faith of conventional believers, and Emily Dickinson's anger, therefore, is directed against her own puzzlement and the double-dealing of religious leaders. It is a frenetic satire that contains a cry of anguish. In the first-person "I know that He exists" (338), the speaker confronts the challenge of death and refers to God with chillingly direct anger. Both poems, however, are ironic. Here, the first stanza declares a firm belief in God's existence, although she can neither hear nor see him. The second stanza explains that he remains hidden in order to make death a blissful ambush, where happiness comes as a surprise. The deliberately excessive joy and the exclamation mark are signs of emerging irony. She has been describing a pleasant game of hide and seek, but she now anticipates that the game may prove deadly and that the fun could turn to terror if death's stare is revealed as being something murderous that brings neither God nor immor-tality. Should this prove so, the amusing game will become a vicious joke, showing God to be a merciless trickster who enjoys watching people's foolish anticipations. Once this dramatic irony is visible, one can see that the first stanza's characterization of God's rareness and man's grossness is ironic. As a vicious trickster, his rareness is a fraud, and if man's lowliness is not rewarded by God, it is merely a sign that people deserve to be cheated. The rhythms of this poem imitate both its deliberativeness and uneasy anticipation. It is as close to blasphemy as Emily Dickinson ever comes in her poems on death, but it does not express an absolute doubt. Rather, it raises the possibility that God may not grant the immortality that we long for.

The borderline between Emily Dickinson's poems in which immortality is painfully doubted and those in which it is merely a question cannot be clearly established, and she often balances between these positions. For example, "Those–dying then" (1551) takes a pragmatic attitude towards the usefulness of faith. Evidently written three or four years before Emily Dickinson's death, this poem reflects on the firm faith of the early nineteenth century, when people were sure that death took them to God's right hand. The amputation of that hand represents the cruel loss of men's faith. The second stanza asserts that without faith people's behavior becomes shallow and petty, and she concludes by declaring that an "ignis fatuus,"– Latin for *false fire*–is better than no illumination–no spiritual guidance or moral anchor. In plain prose, Emily Dickinson's idea seems a bit fatuous. But the poem is effective because it dramatizes, largely through its metaphors of amputation and illumination, the strength that comes with convictions, and contrasts it with an insipid lack of dignity.

The tenderly satirical portrait of a dead woman in "How many times these low feet staggered" (187) skirts the problem of immortality. As in many of her poems about death, the imagery focuses on the stark immobility of the dead, emphasizing their distance from the living. The central scene is a room where a body is laid out for burial, but the speaker's mind ranges back and forth in time. In the first stanza, she looks back at the burdens of life of the dead housewife and then metaphorically describes her stillness. The contrast in her feelings is between relief that the woman is free from her burdens and the present horror of her death. In the second stanza, the speaker asks her listeners or companions to approach the corpse and compare its former, fevered life to its present coolness: the once nimbly active fingers are now stone-like. In the last stanza, attention shifts from the corpse to the room, and the emotion of the speaker complicates. The dull flies and spotted windowpane show that the housewife can no longer keep her house clean. The flies suggest the unclean oppression of death, and the dull sun is a symbol for her extinguished life. By citing the fearless cobweb, the speaker pretends to criticize the dead woman, beginning an irony intensified by a deliberately unjust accusation of indolence – as if the housewife remained dead in order to avoid work. In the last line of the poem, the body is in its grave; this final detail adds a typical Dickinsonian pathos.

"Safe in their Alabaster Chambers" (216) is a similarly constructed but more difficult poem. After Emily Dickinson's sister-in-law, Susan, criticized the second stanza of its first version, Emily Dickinson wrote a different stanza and, later, yet another variant for it. The reader now has the pleasure (or problem) of deciding which second stanza best completes the poem, although one can make a composite version containing all three stanzas, which is what Emily Dickinson's early editors did. We will interpret it as a three-stanza poem. As with "How many times these low feet staggered," its most striking technique is the contrast between the immobility of the dead and the life continuing around them. The tone, however, is solemn rather than partially playful, although slight touches of satire are possible. The first stanza presents a generalized picture of the dead in their graves. The description of the hard whiteness of alabaster monuments or mausoleums begins the poem's stress on the insentience of the dead. Day moves above them but they sleep on, incapable of feeling the softness of coffin linings or the hardness of burial stone. They are "meek members of the resurrection" in that they passively wait for whatever their future may be, although this detail implies that they may eventually awaken in heaven.

In what we will consider the second stanza, the scene widens to the vista of nature surrounding burial grounds. Here, the vigor and cheerfulness of bees and birds emphasizes the stillness and deafness of the dead. The birds are not aware of death, and the former wisdom of the dead, which contrasts to ignorant nature, has perished. In what is our third stanza, Emily Dickinson shifts her scene to the vast surrounding universe, where planets sweep grandly through the heavens. The touch of personification in these lines intensifies the contrast between the continuing universe and the arrested dead. The dropping of diadems stands for the fall of kings, and the reference to Doges, the rulers of medieval Venice, adds an exotic note. The soundless fall of these rulers reminds us again of the dead's insentience and makes the process of cosmic time seem smooth. The disc (enclosing a wide winter landscape) into which fresh snow falls is a simile for this political change and suggests that while such activity is as inevitable as the seasons, it is irrelevant to the dead. This stanza also adds a touch of pathos in that it implies that the dead are equally irrelevant to the world, from whose excitement and variety they are completely cut off. Resurrection has not been mentioned again, and the poem ends on a note of silent awe.

Conflict between doubt and faith looms large in "The last Night that She lived" (1100), perhaps Emily Dickinson's most powerful death scene. The poem is written in second-person plural to emphasize the physical presence and the shared emotions of the witnesses at a death-bed. The past tense shows that the experience has been completed and its details have been intensely remembered. That the night of death is common indicates both that the world goes on despite death and that this persisting commonness in the face of death is offensive to the observers. Nature looks different to the witnesses because they have to face nature's destructiveness and indifference. They see everything with increased sharpness because death makes the world mysterious and precious. After the first two stanzas, the poem devotes four stanzas to contrasts between the situation and the mental state of the dying woman and those of the onlookers. Moving in and out of the death room as a nervous response to their powerlessness, the onlookers become resentful that others may live while this dear woman must die. The jealousy for her is not an envy of her death; it is a jealous defense of her right to live. As the fifth stanza ends, the tense moment of death arrives. The oppressive atmosphere and the spiritually shaken witnesses are made vividly real by the force of the metaphors "narrow time" and "jostled souls." At the moment of death, the dying woman is willing to die – a sign of salvation for the New England Puritan mind and a contrast to the unwillingness of the onlookers to let her die.

The simile of a reed bending to water gives to the woman a fragile beauty and suggests her acceptance of a natural process. In the last stanza the onlookers approach the corpse to arrange it, with formal awe and restrained tenderness. The condensed last two lines gain much of their effect by withholding an expected expression of relief. Instead of going back to life as it was, or affirming their faith in the immortality of a Christian who was willing to die, they move into a time of leisure in which they must strive to "regulate" their beliefs – that is, they must strive to dispel their doubts. The subtle irony of "awful leisure" mocks the condition of still being alive, suggesting that the dead person is more fortunate than the living because she is now relieved of all struggle for faith.

"Because I could not stop for Death" (712) is Emily Dickinson's most anthologized and discussed poem. It deserves such attention, although it is difficult to know how much its problematic nature contributes to this interest. We will briefly summarize the major interpretations before, rather than after, analyzing the poem. Some critics believe that the poem shows death escorting the female speaker to an assured paradise. Others believe that death comes in the form of a deceiver, perhaps even a rapist, to carry her off to destruction. Still others think that the poem leaves the question of her destination open. As does "I heard a Fly buzz – when I died," this poem gains initial force by having its protagonist speak from beyond death. Here, however, dying has largely preceded the action, and its physical aspects are only hinted at. The first stanza presents an apparently cheerful view of a grim subject. Death is kindly. He comes in a vehicle connoting respect or courtship, and he is accompanied by immortality – or at least its promise. The word "stop" can mean to stop by for a person, but it also can mean stopping one's daily activities. With this pun in mind, death's kindness may be seen as ironical, suggesting his grim determination to take the woman despite her occupation with life. Her being alone – or almost alone – with death helps characterize him as a suitor. Death knows no haste because he always has enough power and time. The speaker now acknowledges that she has put her labor and leisure aside; she has given up her claims on life and seems pleased with her exchange of life for death's civility, a civility appropriate for a suitor but an ironic quality of a force that has no need for rudeness.

The third stanza creates a sense of motion and of the separation between the living and the dead. Children go on with life's conflicts and games, which are now irrelevant to the dead woman. The vitality of nature which is embodied in the grain and the sun is also irrelevant to her state; it makes a frightening contrast. However, in the fourth stanza, she becomes troubled by her separation from nature and by what seems to be a physical threat. She realizes that the sun is passing them rather than they the sun, suggesting both that she has lost the power of independent movement, and that time is leaving her behind. Her dress and her scarf are made of frail materials and the wet chill of evening, symbolizing the coldness of death, assaults her. Some critics believe that she wears the white robes of the bride of Christ and is headed towards a celestial marriage. In the fifth stanza, the body is deposited in the grave, whose representation as a swelling in the ground portends its sinking. The flatness of its roof and its low roof-supports reinforce the atmosphere of dissolution and may symbolize the swiftness with which the dead are forgotten. The last stanza implies that the carriage with driver and guest are still traveling. If it is centuries since the body was deposited, then the soul is moving on without the body. That first day felt longer than the succeeding centuries because during it, she experienced the shock of death. Even then, she knew that the destination was eternity, but the poem does not tell if that eternity is filled with anything more than the blankness into which her senses are dissolving. Emily Dickinson may intend paradise to be the woman's destination, but the conclusion withholds a description of what immortality may be like. The presence of immortality in the carriage may be part of a mocking game or it may indicate some kind of real promise. Since interpretation of some of the details is problematic, readers must decide for themselves what the poem's dominant tone is.

The borderline between Emily Dickinson's treatment of death as having an uncertain outcome and her affirmation of immortality cannot be clearly defined. The epigrammatic "The Bustle in a House" (1078) makes a more definite affirmation of immortality than the poems just discussed, but its tone is still grim. If we wanted to make a narrative sequence of two of Emily Dickinson's poems about death, we could place this one after "The last Night that She lived." "The Bustle in a House" at first appears to be an objective description of a household following the death of a dear person. It is only the morning after, but already there is the bustle of everyday activity. The word "bustle" implies a brisk busyness, a return to the normality and the order shattered by the departure of the dying. Industry is ironically joined to solemnity, but rather than mocking industry, Emily Dickinson shows how such busyness is an attempt to subdue grief. The second stanza makes a bold reversal, whereby the domestic activities – which the first stanza implies are physical – become a sweeping up not of house but of heart. Unlike household things, heart and love are not put away temporarily. They are put away until we join the dead in eternity. The last line affirms the existence of immortality, but the emphasis on the distance in time (for the dead) also stresses death's mystery. Viewed as the morning after "The last Night that She lived," this poem depicts everyday activity as a ritualization of the struggle for belief. Such a continuity also helps bring out the wistfulness of "The Bustle in a House." Few of Emily Dickinson's poems illustrate so concisely her mixing of the commonplace and the elevated, and her deft sense of everyday psychology.

"A Clock stopped" (287) mixes the domestic and the elevated in order to communicate the pain of losing dear people and also to suggest the distance of the dead from the living. The poem is an allegory in which a clock represents a person who has just died. The first stanza contrasts the all-important "clock," a once-living human being, with a trivial mechanical clock. This prepares us for the angry remark that men's skills can do nothing to bring back the dead. Geneva is the home of the most famous clockmakers and also the place where Calvinist Christianity was born. The reference to a puppet reveals that this is a cuckoo clock with dancing figures. This image of the puppet suggests the triviality of the mere body, as opposed to the soul that has fled. The second stanza rehearses the process of dying. The clock is a trinket because the dying body is a mere plaything of natural processes. A painful death strikes rapidly, and instead of remaining a creature of time, the "clock-person" enters the timeless and perfect realm of eternity, symbolized here, as in other Emily Dickinson poems, by noon. In the third stanza, the poem's speaker becomes sardonic about the powerlessness of doctors, and possibly ministers, to revive the dead, and then turns with a strange detachment to the owner – friend, relative, lover – who begs the dead to return.

But whatever is left of vitality in the aspects of the dead person refuses to exert itself. The residues of time that this "clock-person" incorporates suddenly expand into the decades that separate it from the living; these decades are the time between the present and the shopman's death, when he will join the "clock-person" in eternity. The arrogance of the decades belongs to the dead because they have achieved the perfect noon of eternity and can look with scorn at merely finite concerns.

In the early poem "Just lost, when I was saved!" (160), Emily Dickinson expresses joyful assurance of immortality by dramatizing her regret about a return to life after she – or an imagined speaker – almost died and received many vivid and thrilling hints about a world beyond death. Each of the first three lines makes a pronouncement about the false joy of being saved from a death which is actually desirable. Her real joy lay in her brief contact with eternity. When she recovers her life, she hears the realm of eternity express disappointment, for it shared her true joy in her having almost arrived there. The second stanza reveals her awe of the realm which she skirted, the adventure being represented in metaphors of sailing, sea, and shore. As a "pale reporter," she is weak from illness and able to give only a vague description of what lies beyond the seals of heaven. In the third and fourth stanzas, she declares in chanted prayer that when next she approaches eternity she wants to stay and witness in detail everything which she has only glimpsed. The last three lines are a celebration of the timelessness of eternity. She uses the image of the ponderous movements of vast amounts of earthly time to emphasize that her happy eternity lasts even longer – it lasts forever.

"Those not live yet" (1454) may be Emily Dickinson's strongest single affirmation of immortality, but it has found little favor with anthologists, probably because of its dense grammar. The writing is elliptical to an extreme, suggesting almost a strained trance in the speaker, as if she could barely express what has become for her the most important thing. The first two lines assert that people are not yet alive if they do not believe that they will live for a second time – that is, after death. The next two lines turn the adverb "again" into a noun and declare that the notion of immortality as an "again" is based on a false separation of life and an afterlife. The truth, rather, is that life is part of a single continuity. The next three lines analogize death to a connection between two parts of the same reality. The ship that strikes against the sea's bottom when passing through a channel will make its way over that brief grounding and enter a continuation of the same sea. This sea is consciousness, and death is merely a painful hesitation as we move from one phase of the sea to the next. The last three lines contain an image of the realm beyond the present life as being pure consciousness without the costume of the body, and the word "disc" suggests timeless expanse as well as a mutuality between consciousness and all existence.

"Behind Me – dips Eternity" (721) strives for an equally strong affirmation of immortality, but it reveals more pain than "Those not live yet" and perhaps some doubt. In the first stanza, the speaker is trapped in life between the immeasurable past and the immeasurable future. Death is represented as the dark of early morning which will turn into the light of paradise. The second stanza celebrates immortality as the realm of God's timelessness. Rather than celebrating the trinity, Emily Dickinson first insists on God's single perpetual being, which diversifies itself in divine duplicates. This difficult passage probably means that each person's achievement of immortality makes him part of God. The phrase "they say" and the chant-like insistence of the first two stanzas suggest a person trying to convince herself of these truths. The pain expressed in the final stanza illuminates this uncertainty. The miracle behind her is the endless scope of time. The miracle before her is the promise of resurrection, and the miracle between is the quality of her own being – probably what God has given her of Himself – that guarantees that she will live again. However, the last three lines portray her life as a living hell, presumably of conflict, denial, and alienation. If this is the case, we can see why she is yearning for an immortal life. But she still fears that her present "midnight" neither promises nor deserves to be changed in heaven. These doubts, of course, are only implications. The poem is primarily an indirect prayer that her hopes may be fulfilled.

It is hard to locate a developing pattern in Emily Dickinson's poems on death, immortality, and religious questions. Clearly, Emily Dickinson wanted to believe in God and immortality, and she often thought that life and the universe would make little sense without them. Possibly her faith increased in her middle and later years; certainly one can cite certain poems, including "Those not live yet," as signs of an inner conversion. However, serious expressions of doubt persist, apparently to the very end.

Emily Dickinson treats religious faith directly in the epigrammatic " 'Faith' is a fine invention" (185), whose four lines paradoxically maintain that faith is an acceptable invention when it is based on concrete perception, which suggests that it is merely a way of claiming that orderly or pleasing things follow a principle. When we can see no reason for faith, she next declares, it would be good to have tools to uncover real evidence. Here, she finds it hard to believe in the unseen, although many of her best poems struggle for just such belief. Although "Drowning is not so pitiful" (1718) is a poem about death, it has a kind of naked and sarcastic skepticism which emphasizes the general problem of faith. The poem's directness and intensity lead one to suspect that its basis is personal suffering and a fear for the loss of self, despite its insistence on death as the central challenge to faith. Its first four lines describe a drowning person desperately clinging to life. In the next four lines, the process of drowning is horrible, and the horror is partly attributed to a fear of God. The last four lines bitingly imply that people are not telling the truth when they affirm their faith that they will see God and be happy after death. These lines make God seem cruel. Emily Dickinson's uncharacteristic lack of charity suggests that she is thinking of mankind's tendency as a whole, rather than of specific dying people.

Emily Dickinson sent "The Bible is an antique Volume" (1545) to her twenty-two year-old nephew, Ned, when he was ill. At this time, she was about fifty-two and had only four more years to live. The poem might be less surprising if it were a product of Emily Dickinson's earlier years, although perhaps she was remembering some of her own reactions to the Bible during her youth. The first three lines echo standard explanations of the Bible's origin as holy doctrine, and the mocking tone implies skepticism. It then quickly summarizes and domesticates scenes and characters from the Bible as if they were everyday examples of virtue and sin. Lines nine through twelve are the core of the criticism, for they express anger against the preaching of self-righteous teachers. In conclusion, she pleads for literature with more color and presumably with more varied material and less narrow values. The poem may be a complaint against a Puritan interpretation of the Bible and against Puritan skepticism about secular literature. On the other hand, it may merely be a playful expression of a fanciful and joking mood.

Given the variety of Emily Dickinson's attitudes and moods, it is easy to select evidence to "prove" that she held certain views. But such patterns can be dogmatic and distorting. Emily Dickinson's final thoughts on many subjects are hard to know. With this caution in mind, we can glance at the trenchant "Apparently with no surprise" (1624), also written within a few years of Emily Dickinson's death. The flower here may seem to stand for merely natural things, but the emphatic personification implies that God's way of afflicting the lowly flowers resembles his treatment of man. The happy flower does not expect a blow and feels no surprise when it is struck, but this is only "apparently." Perhaps it does suffer. The image of frost beheading the flower implies an abrupt and unthinking brutality. The personification of Frost as an assassin contradicts the notion of its acting accidentally. Nature in the guise of the sun takes no notice of the cruelty, and God seems to approve of the natural process. This implies that God and natural process are identical, and that they are either indifferent, or cruel, to living things, including man. The subtleties and implications of this poem illustrate the difficulties that the skeptical mind encounters in dealing with a universe in which God's presence is not easily demonstrated. The poem is strangely, and magnificently, detached and cold. It makes an interesting contrast to Emily Dickinson's more personal expressions of doubt and to her strongest affirmations of faith.

BRIEF COMMENTS ON FORTY ADDITIONAL POEMS

To conclude, we offer one-sentence comments on forty poems not analyzed or mentioned in these Notes. Since we have already suggested a variety of thematic patterns among Dickinson's poems, we are avoiding classification of these additional poems, leaving the reader free to relate them to Dickinson's themes. They are arranged here in alphabetical order. These brief comments do not attempt definitive or assured interpretations, nor do they mention alternate views.

"A Light exists in Spring" (812): A special light on the landscape during spring conveys a feeling of urgency and vitality, and its departure leaves the viewer with a sense of restive deprivation. "A Word made Flesh is seldom" (1651): The speaker wishes that the experience of expressing one's feelings adequately, which is like the act of God taking on flesh, could come more frequently. "A Wounded Deer — leaps highest" (165): Various kinds of suffering produce apparently joyful compensations which take the form of defenses against real pain. "Ample make this Bed" (829): Instructions for the correct frame of mind about burying people are given in a sinister manner, suggesting uncertainty about the destiny of the dead. "As the Starved Maelstrom laps the Navies" (872): The speaker compares her aggressive desire to consume something exotic, probably a beloved person, with the behavior of starved creatures.

"Civilization – spurns – the Leopard!" (492): A leopard, symbolizing the poet-speaker, was oppressed and rejected by her conventional society and deserves pity for her inability to live according to her natural desires. "Death is the supple Suitor" (1445): Death takes the form of a dishonest lover and woos his victims to a secret and silent realm. "Did the Harebell loose her girdle" (213): As an allegory drawn from nature may suggest, after women yield their virginity to estimable men, the promised rewards and the stature of the men will probably be diminished. "God is a distant – stately Lover" (357): The Christian idea that God needed to become Christ in order to win men over is satirically compared and contrasted to Miles Standish's use of John Alden to carry his marriage suit to Priscilla, in Longfellow's narrative poem *The Courtship of Miles Standish*. " 'Heavenly Father' – take to thee" (1461): We pray that God will receive us in heaven despite our sins, but such a prayer neglects the likelihood that the creator made us sinful.

"He fumbles at your Soul" (315): The power of a magnificently eloquent speaker (or minister or writer) to transform his audience's feelings is compared to music, thunderbolts, and forest winds. "He preached upon 'Breadth' till it argued him narrow" (1207): A liberal minister makes such exaggerated claims for his broad-mindedness and grasp of truth that he reveals insincerity, lack of faith, and pretentiousness. " 'Hope' is the thing with feathers" (254): Hope has various characteristics of a courageous bird, the most important being its total self-reliance or sourcelessness. "How happy is the little Stone" (1510): In its complete independence and security, a small stone provides a model for man's spiritual self-sufficiency. "I breathed enough to take the Trick" (272): The speaker learned to function adequately when she had a supportive environment, but now that she lives with deprivation she manages to survive by sheer nerve.

"I can wade Grief" (252): The speaker finds pain easier to endure and more creative than joy, for she has learned that unchallenging circumstances weaken people, whereas heavy burdens strengthen them. "I found the words to every thought" (581): The speaker is taking both pain and pleasure in illustrating her feeling that she can find no words for her most valuable experience, possibly some sense of

personal or cosmic wholeness. "I got so I could take his name" (293):
The speaker rehearses her agonizing and slow adjustment to a forci-
ble separation from a beloved man and continues to address prayers
about her situation to a deity who seems unlikely to care about her
suffering. "I've seen a Dying Eye" (547): The speaker remembers
watching a dying person whose slowly closing eyes revealed nothing
of whatever happy future they could see. "Of God we ask one favor"
(1601): People ask God to forgive their sins even if their only sense of
sin is awareness of God's accusation, and they are thereby compelled
to criticize an earthly happiness which they would like to have per-
petuated in heaven.

"One dignity delays for all" (98): Everyone, no matter how low
can look forward to dying as something that will elevate him to a
high rank, presumably a spiritual existence in heaven. "One need not
be a Chamber – to be Haunted" (670): Psychological or spiritual
threats inside people are greater dangers than threat of ghosts or of
physical aggression, though most people take the opposite view
"Myself was formed – a Carpenter" (488): The speaker's earnest and
elevated view of her destiny as a carpenter suggests that she is talk-
ing about the way in which someone belittles her sacred poetic gift
by wanting her to subdue it to convention. "Not with a Club, the
Heart is broken" (1304): The speaker externalizes an inner drama of
self-accusation to show the crushing power of shame in human life
"Pain – has an Element of Blank" (650): A major ingredient of pain
presumably a pain permeating all of one's being, is its loss of any
time-sense about its own engulfment.

"She lay as if at play" (369): The body of a recently dead girl
shows such vivid signs of its recent vitality that it is hard not to
believe that she is merely asleep and will soon awaken. "Some keep
the Sabbath going to Church" (324): The speaker indirectly offers
various reasons why she finds more vividness and joy in performing
Sunday worship in a natural setting near her home than she would in
celebrating it by attending church services. "Split the Lark – and
you'll find the Music" (861): Addressing a dear person who seems to
doubt the speaker's absolute devotion, she insists that exposing the
torment inside her would prove her sincerity. "The Admirations –
and Contempts – of time" (906): When we are on the verge of dying
we can see that the true meaning of time is that it shows the conditions of mortality and immortality to be fused together through the

ower of God. "The Bat is dun, with wrinkled Wings" (1575): The un-
pleasant but relatively harmless physical aspects of bats are puzzling,
but we should assume that God acts with goodwill in making such a
strange creature.

"The Brain, within its Groove" (56): The human brain, standing
for the individual personality or for psychic wholeness, functions
smoothly unless some part of it breaks down, in which case the
damage to the whole is almost irreversible. "The Lamp burns sure—
within" (233): The human spirit is like a lamp tended and fed by outside forces, but if these forces fail it, it can miraculously go on just as
it previously did. "The Malay—took the Pearl" (452): The speaker
compares her timid self to a primitive person who is able to achieve
satisfactions that frighten her but who has little of her appreciation
for such achievements. "The soul has Bandaged moments" (512): The
soul, a person much like the poet, goes through periods of bitter self-
condemnation and then of joyful release, but when she returns to the
oppressed state, things are worse than ever. "The Soul's Superior in-
stants" (306): During its best moments, the sensitive soul revels in its
detachment from everything and in its complete self-sufficiency;
such realizations are identical with the sense of immortality.

"There is a pain—so utter" (599): Some kinds of engulfing pain
protect the sufferer from distintegration by making him numb to the
causes and nature of the pain. "Three times—we parted—breath—
and I" (598): The speaker was three times threatened with the complete destruction of her spirit, but after giving up hope of outside
help she was saved by an inner transformation or rebirth. "To fight
aloud, is very brave" (126): The speaker celebrates the act of endur-
ing spiritual suffering, and she is sure that people who practice the
former will be elevated in heaven. "To hang our head—ostensibly"
(105): The fact that many people pretend to have faith and humility
that they discover they do not really feel is evidence that a person being addressed by this poem does not really believe in his frail arguments for some articles of faith. "What Inn is this" (115): Having arrived in the realm of death, the speaker is satirically curious about a
lack of vitality in its residents and caretakers, for she had expected to
find miraculous resurrection.

QUESTIONS FOR REVIEW AND WRITING

1. Why is a good general knowledge of Emily Dickinson's life useful for interpreting her poems?
2. How can knowledge of Emily Dickinson's life be misused in interpreting her poems?
3. Compare and contrast "We play at Paste" (320) and "Essential Oils – are wrung" (675).
4. Discuss the use of abstractions as vivid metaphors in "I dwell in Possibility" (657).
5. Compare and contrast the use of animals as symbols in Dickinson's love poems.
6. Discuss the relationship between deprivation and fulfillment in Dickinson's love poems.
7. Compare and contrast Dickinson's joyful and melancholy responses to nature.
8. Discuss the use of metaphors in Dickinson's nature scenes.
9. Discuss Dickinson's various tones, from ecstatic to anguished in showing how rebirth can come from suffering.
10. Discuss the figure of the speaker as a little girl in Dickinson's poems.
11. Offer detailed arguments for the varying interpretations of "Because I could not stop for Death" (712).
12. Compare and contrast the changes of mood dramatized in "This world is not Conclusion" (501) and "I know that He exists" (338).
13. Discuss the figure of death as a lover in Dickinson's poems.
14. Compare and contrast Dickinson's first-person and third-person death scenes.
15. Discuss in detail your reasons for disagreeing with any whole interpretation of a poem made in these Notes.

SELECTED BIBLIOGRAPHY

ANDERSON, CHARLES R. *Emily Dickinson's Poetry: Stairway of Surprise*. New York: Holt, Rinehart, and Winston, 1960. Careful analysis of over one hundred poems.

BLAKE, CAESAR R. AND CARLTON F. WELLS, EDS. *The Recognition of Emily Dickinson: Selected Criticism Since 1890*. Ann Arbor

University of Michigan Press, 1964. Collection of critical reviews, essays, and excerpts from books, arranged chronologically. Especially valuable for early critical views of Dickinson.

HASE, RICHARD. *Emily Dickinson.* New York: William Sloane Associates, 1951. Competent critical biography based on pre-Johnson texts. Very qualified admiration for poems.

ODY, JOHN. *After Great Pain: The Inner Life of Emily Dickinson.* Cambridge, Mass.: Harvard University Press, 1971. Highly speculative psychoanalytic study interrelating life and poems.

AVIS, THOMAS F., ED. *14 By Dickinson.* Chicago: Scott, Foresman, 1964. Collection of explications of fourteen well known poems.

ELPI, ALBERT J. *Emily Dickinson: The Mind of the Poet.* Cambridge, Mass.: Harvard University Press, 1965. Excellent study of Dickinson's major ideas, their sources, and interrelations.

RIFFITH, CLARK. *The Long Shadow: Emily Dickinson's Tragic Poetry.* Princeton University Press, 1964. Largely psychological treatment of Dickinson's most anguished poems as her greatest accomplishment. Exaggerates her skepticism.

OHNSON, THOMAS H. *Emily Dickinson: An Interpretive Biography.* Cambridge, Mass.: Harvard University Press, 1955. First critical biography based on Johnson text.

EYDA, JAY. *The Years and Hours of Emily Dickinson.* New Haven: Yale University Press, 1960. 2 vols. Huge compilation of documents bearing on Dickinson's life; partly duplicates edition of her letters.

INDBERG-SEYERSTED, BRITA. *The Voice of the Poet: Aspects of Style in the Poetry of Emily Dickinson.* Cambridge, Mass.: Harvard University Press, 1968. Systematic study of Dickinson's language habits, including prosody.

PICKARD, JOHN. *Emily Dickinson: An Introduction and Interpretation* New York: Holt, Rinehart, and Winston, 1968. Probably the best brief general introduction.

ROSENBAUM, S. P. *A Concordance to the Poems of Emily Dickinson* Ithaca, New York: Cornell University Press, 1964. Compute assisted concordance to variorum edition of poems. Invaluable for locating individual poems and for studying Dickinson's use of specific words.

SEWALL, RICHARD B. *The Life of Emily Dickinson*, 2 vols. New York Farrar, Straus and Giroux, 1974. A biography. Hugely inclusive of facts and carefully non-dogmatic in its interpretation.

_____. *Emily Dickinson: A Collection of Critical Essays.* Engle wood Cliffs: Prentice Hall, 1963. Excellent collection of critical essays and excerpts from books.

WARD, THEODORA. *The Capsule of the Mind: Chapters in the Life o Emily Dickinson.* Cambridge, Mass.: Harvard University Press 1961. Interrelated essays on key stages of Dickinson's inner life sharp insights without technical psychological vocabulary.

WEISBUCH, ROBERT. *Emily Dickinson's Poetry.* Chicago: University o Chicago Press, 1975. Fine study of how Dickinson's represen tational and symbolic techniques relate to problems of interpre tation.

WHICHER, GEORGE F. *This Was a Poet: A Critical Biography of Emil; Dickinson.* New York: Charles Scribner's Sons, 1939. The pio neering scholarly biography. Still useful for critical insights and commentary on background of Dickinson's ideas.

INDEX OF FIRST LINES

NOTES

NOTES